First World War
and Army of Occupation
War Diary
France, Belgium and Germany

21 DIVISION
110 Infantry Brigade,
Brigade Machine Gun Company
and Brigade Trench Mortar Battery
28 October 1914 - 28 February 1918

WO95/2165/4-5

The Naval & Military Press Ltd
www.nmarchive.com
Published in association with The National Archives

Published by

The Naval & Military Press Ltd

Unit 10 Ridgewood Industrial Park,

Uckfield, East Sussex,

TN22 5QE England

Tel: +44 (0) 1825 749494

www.naval-military-press.com

www.nmarchive.com

This diary has been reprinted in facsimile from the original. Any imperfections are inevitably reproduced and the quality may fall short of modern type and cartographic standards.

© Crown Copyright
Images reproduced by permission of The National Archives, London, England, 2015.

Contents

Document type	Place/Title	Date From	Date To
Heading	WO95/2165/4		
Heading	21st Division 110th Infy Bde 110th Machine Gun Coy. Jly 1916-Feb 1918		
Heading	110th Inf. Bde. 21st Div. Company transferred with Bde. from 37th Div. 7.7.16 War Diary 110th Machine Gun Company July 1916		
Miscellaneous	Appendices "A" "B" & "C".		
Operation(al) Order(s)	Operation Order No. 5 by Capt. W.W. Ashcroft. Comg 195 M.G. Coy. Appendix 5	21/10/1917	21/10/1917
Miscellaneous	Headquarters 110 Inf Brigade 110/A/17	26/07/1916	26/07/1916
Miscellaneous	Battle of the Somme.July 1916 no 2 Section 110th M.G. Coy	25/07/1916	25/07/1916
Miscellaneous	Battle of the Somme Infy 1916 no 4 Section 110th M.G. Coy.		
Heading	War Diary		
War Diary	Humbercamps	01/07/1916	03/07/1916
War Diary	La Bazeque	04/07/1916	06/07/1916
War Diary	Talmas	07/07/1916	07/07/1916
War Diary	Lequesnoit	08/07/1916	10/07/1916
War Diary	Meaulte	10/07/1916	10/07/1916
War Diary	Fricourt	10/07/1916	13/07/1916
War Diary	Mametz Wood	14/07/1916	16/07/1916
War Diary	Fricourt Wood	17/07/1916	17/07/1916
War Diary	Ribemont	18/09/1916	20/09/1916
War Diary	Lequesnoit	21/01/1916	22/07/1916
War Diary	Gouy	23/07/1916	24/07/1916
War Diary		25/07/1916	25/07/1916
War Diary	Lattre St Quentin	26/07/1916	27/07/1916
War Diary	Arras	28/07/1916	31/07/1916
Heading	110th Brigade. 21st Division. 110th Brigade Machine Gun Company August 1916		
War Diary	Arras	01/08/1916	31/08/1916
Operation(al) Order(s)	Operation Order No. 14 by Capt A S Bowdern Commdg 110 M.G. Coy		
Operation(al) Order(s)	Machine Gun Coy Operation Order No 34		
Operation(al) Order(s)	Operation Order No. 3A		
Operation(al) Order(s)	Operation Order No. 4		
Heading	110th Brigade. 21st Division. 110th Brigade Machine Gun Company September 1916		
War Diary	Arras	01/09/1916	03/09/1916
War Diary	Montenescourt	04/09/1916	04/09/1916
War Diary	Berlencourt	05/09/1916	13/09/1916
War Diary	Frevent	14/09/1916	14/09/1916
War Diary	Heilly	14/09/1916	15/09/1916
War Diary	Dernancourt	15/09/1916	15/09/1916
War Diary	Fricourt Camp	16/09/1916	16/09/1916
War Diary	Pommiers Redoubt	17/09/1916	18/09/1916
War Diary	Montauban	19/09/1916	30/09/1916
Operation(al) Order(s)	Operation Order No. 4A Appendix "A"		

Operation(al) Order(s)	Operation Order No. 5 by Capt a H. Bowden Comndg 110 M.G. Coy Appendix "B"		
Miscellaneous	Synopsis of Operation of 110 Machine Gun Company from 6 pm 24.9.16 to midnight 1/2 Oct. Appendix "C"	24/09/1916	24/09/1916
Heading	War Diary 110 Machine Gun Coy from Oct 1st-31st 1916 Volume 8		
War Diary	Gueudecourt	01/10/1916	01/10/1916
War Diary	Montauban	02/10/1916	02/10/1916
War Diary	Dernancourt	03/10/1916	04/10/1916
War Diary	Longpre	05/10/1916	05/10/1916
War Diary	Longuet	06/10/1916	07/10/1916
War Diary	Bethune	08/10/1916	08/10/1916
War Diary	Fouquereuil	09/10/1916	10/10/1916
War Diary	Vermelles	11/10/1916	31/10/1916
Heading	War Diary of 110th Machine Gun Company from 1st November 1916 to 30th November 1916		
War Diary	Vermelles	01/11/1916	30/11/1916
Heading	War Diary of 110 Machine Gun Company from 1st December 1916 to 31st December 1916 Vol.11		
War Diary	Vermelles	01/12/1916	14/12/1916
War Diary	Bethune	15/12/1916	20/12/1916
War Diary	Auchel	21/12/1916	31/12/1916
Operation(al) Order(s)	Operation Order No. 18 by Major A.H. Bowden. Commanding 110 Machine Gun Company Appendix "A"		
Operation(al) Order(s)	Operation Order No. 2B by Major A.H. Bowden, Commanding 110 Machine Gun Company Appendix "B"		
Heading	War Diary of 110th Machine Gun Company from 1st January 1917 to 31st January 1917 Vol 12		
War Diary	Auchel	01/01/1917	25/01/1917
War Diary	Proven	28/01/1917	28/01/1917
War Diary	Briel	29/01/1917	13/02/1917
War Diary	Bethune	14/02/1917	14/02/1917
War Diary	Vermelles	15/02/1916	28/02/1916
Miscellaneous	Reference Operation Orders No. B.4 Issued to-day, the following alterations will be made. Appendix "A"		
Operation(al) Order(s)	Operation Orders No. B.4 by Major A.H. Bowden Commanding 110 Machine Gun Company		
Heading	War Diary of 110 Machine Gun Company from 1st March 1917 to 31st March 1917 Vol. 14		
War Diary	Vermelles	01/03/1917	02/03/1917
War Diary	Noyelles	03/03/1917	16/03/1917
War Diary	Vermelles	17/03/1917	26/03/1917
War Diary	Noyelles	27/03/1917	29/03/1917
War Diary	Humbercamp	30/03/1917	31/03/1917
Operation(al) Order(s)	Operation Orders No. B.6 by Major A.H. Bowden. Commanding 110 Machine Gun Company.		
War Diary	Humbercamp	01/04/1917	02/04/1917
War Diary	Hamelincourt	03/04/1917	30/04/1917
Heading	War Diary of 110 Machine Gun Company from 1st May 1917 to 31st May 1917 Vol. 16		
War Diary	Boyelles	01/05/1917	01/05/1917
War Diary	Hinden Burg Line	02/05/1917	04/05/1917
War Diary	St Leger	05/05/1917	10/05/1917
War Diary	Bienvillers	11/05/1917	12/05/1917

Type	Location/Description	Start	End
Miscellaneous	Bienvillers Au Bois	13/05/1917	31/05/1917
Miscellaneous	110 Machine Gun Company		
Heading	War Diary of 110th Machine Gun Coy from June 1st 1917 to June 30th 1917 Vol 17		
War Diary	Bienvillers Au Bois	01/06/1917	01/06/1917
War Diary	Moyenneville	02/06/1917	06/06/1917
War Diary	St. Leger	07/06/1917	19/06/1917
War Diary	Moyenneville	20/06/1917	20/06/1917
War Diary	Blairville	20/06/1917	30/06/1917
Miscellaneous	Operation Orders by Major A.H. Bowden, Commanding 110th Machine Gun Company. Appendix I.		
Miscellaneous	Operation Order by Major A.H. Bowden, Commanding 110 Machine Gun Company. Appendix 2.		
Operation(al) Order(s)	Reference 110th Brigade Operation Orders No. 69 Machine Gun Appendix. Appendix 3	15/06/1917	15/06/1917
Operation(al) Order(s)	Reference 110th Brigade Operation Orders No. 69 Machine Gun Appendix.		
War Diary	Blairville	01/07/1917	01/07/1917
War Diary	Moyenneville	02/07/1917	08/07/1917
War Diary	St Leger	09/07/1917	31/07/1917
Miscellaneous	Operation Orders by Lieut T.D. Halliman Commanding 110 Machine Gun Company.		
Miscellaneous	Operation Orders by Major A.H. Bowden Commanding 110 Machine Gun Company.	07/07/1917	07/07/1917
War Diary	St Leger	01/08/1917	01/08/1917
War Diary	Moyenneville	02/08/1917	25/08/1917
War Diary	Monchiet	26/08/1917	26/08/1917
War Diary	Izel-Les-Hameau	27/08/1917	08/09/1917
War Diary	Dickebusch	09/09/1917	16/09/1917
War Diary	Izel Lez Hameau Dickebusch	17/09/1917	20/09/1917
War Diary	Dickebusch	21/09/1917	23/09/1917
War Diary	Meteren	24/09/1917	28/09/1917
War Diary	Micmac Camp	29/09/1917	29/09/1917
War Diary	Ridge Wood	30/09/1917	30/09/1917
Operation(al) Order(s)	110th Machine Gun Company Operation Order No. 11 Appendix "A"	18/09/1917	18/09/1917
Miscellaneous	Machine Guns Table "A"		
Miscellaneous	Detailed Orders 110th Machine Gun Company Appendix "A"		
Miscellaneous	Appendix "B" Administration		
Miscellaneous	Casualties Sustained by 110th Machine Gun Company during Period 18th Septr-22nd Sept 1917	22/09/1917	22/09/1917
Miscellaneous	Report On the action of 110th Machine Gun Company Whilst attached to the 39th Division for Operations ON September 20th	24/09/1917	24/09/1917
Miscellaneous	Tactical and Technical Lessons learnt during Operations of 20/9/17	20/09/1917	20/09/1917
War Diary	Ridge Wood Camp Mr Dickebusch	01/10/1917	02/10/1917
War Diary	Polygon Wood	03/10/1917	05/10/1917
War Diary	Ridge Wood Camp	06/10/1917	06/10/1917
War Diary	Polygon Wood	06/10/1917	11/10/1917
War Diary	Wardrecques	12/10/1917	20/10/1917
War Diary	Dickebusch	21/10/1917	23/10/1917
War Diary	Chateau	24/10/1917	24/10/1917
War Diary	Segard	28/10/1914	28/10/1914

War Diary	Polygon Wood	29/10/1917	31/10/1917
Operation(al) Order(s)	110th Machine Gun Company Operation Order No. 12. Appendix "A"		
Miscellaneous	Details Orders-110th Machine Gun Company Appendix "A"		
Miscellaneous	Appendix "A"		
Miscellaneous	Appendix "B"		
Heading	War Diary of 110th Machine Gun Company 1st to 30th November 1917. Vol 22		
War Diary	Polygon Wood	01/11/1917	05/11/1917
War Diary	Chateau Segard	06/11/1917	16/11/1917
War Diary	Reninghelst	17/11/1917	18/11/1917
War Diary	Doulieu	19/11/1917	19/11/1917
War Diary	La Couronne	20/11/1917	20/11/1917
War Diary	Vendin-Lez-Bethune	21/11/1917	21/11/1917
War Diary	Hersin Coupigny	22/11/1917	24/11/1917
War Diary	Hersin Houvelin	26/11/1917	30/11/1917
Heading	War Diary of 110th Machine Gun Company for December 1917 Vol. 23		
War Diary	Tincourt	01/12/1917	02/12/1917
War Diary	Epehy	03/12/1917	09/12/1917
War Diary	Longavesnes	10/12/1917	17/12/1917
War Diary	Epehy	18/12/1917	26/12/1917
War Diary	Longavesnes	27/12/1917	31/12/1917
Miscellaneous	Appendix "A" 110th Machine Gun Company.		
Heading	Original War Diary of 110th Machine Gun Company for January 1918 Vol. 24		
War Diary	Longavesnes	01/01/1918	03/01/1918
War Diary	Epehy	04/01/1918	13/01/1918
War Diary	Longavesnes	14/01/1918	14/01/1918
War Diary	Saulcourt Wood	15/01/1918	21/01/1918
War Diary	Epehy	22/01/1918	29/01/1918
War Diary	Saulcourt Wood	30/01/1918	31/01/1918
Heading	War Diary of 110th Machine Gun Company for February 1918 Vol. 25		
War Diary	Saulcourt Wood	01/02/1918	07/02/1918
War Diary	Epehy Right Sector	08/02/1918	15/02/1918
War Diary	Hamel	16/02/1918	28/02/1918
Heading	WO95/2165/5		
Heading	110th Brigade. 21st Division. 110th Trench Mortar Battery August 1916		
War Diary		31/07/1916	04/08/1916
War Diary		02/08/1916	18/08/1916
War Diary		18/08/1916	18/08/1916
War Diary		14/08/1916	31/08/1916

3095/2/65/4

21ST DIVISION
110TH INFY BDE

110TH MACHINE GUN COY.
JLY 1916 - FEB 1918

110th Inf.Bde.
21st Div.

Company transferred with Bde. from 37th Div.
7.7.16.

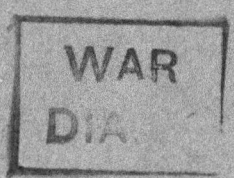

110th MACHINE GUN COMPANY.

J U L Y

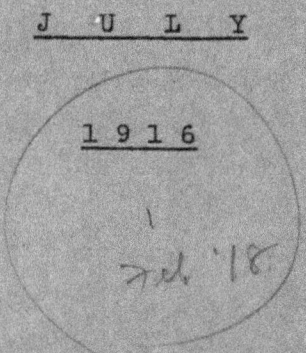

1 9 1 6

Attached:

Appendices A, B & C.
(Reports on Operations).

A P P E N D I C E S   "A", "B" & "C".

Reports on Operations by O.C. Company,
and O.Cs. Nos. 2 & 4 Sections.

APPENDIX 5

Operation Order No 5
by
Capt. W.W. Ashcroft
Comd 195 M.G. Coy.

Secret
Copy No. 6
APPENDIX.5.

Map Ref. {La Bassee 36ᵃ N.W.1 }
         {Richbourg 36 S.W.3 } 1-10.100

1. The 195 M.G. Coy. with 12 guns will relieve the 7ᵗʰ M.G.Coy with 16 guns in the GIVENCHY sector of the Division on the afternoon of the 21ˢᵗ inst.

2. The 7ᵗʰ Coy. will hand over 4 guns complete in position No 9-10.11+12 and the 195 M.G.Coy will provide 16 gun teams of 3 men & 1 N.C.O. each except 1 team of 3 men from No 3 Section.

3. Sections will provide teams as follows:-
   No 1. Section under Lᵗ Brutton will take over 5 guns in the right sub. sector in position Nos 1.2.3. 4+5 with H.Q. at MOAT FARM
   No 2 Section under 2/Lᵗ HIND will take over 5 guns in centre sub. sector in position No 6.7. 8.9 +10 with H.Q. at A 2 D 7. 4.
   No 3 Section under 2/Lᵗ WILKINS will take over 6 guns in the left sub sector in positions Nos 11.12.13.14 15+16 with H.Q. at DEAD COW FARM.
   No 2 Section will hand over one gun complete to No.1. Section

4. Tripods & Belt Boxes will be taken over and **Reliefs** will be reported immediately when complete and Receipts for all tripods (noting condition) belt boxes, S.A.A. Trench stores, Maps, telephone wires &c taken over will be sent to advanced Coy. H.Q. at LE PLANTIN with 1ˢᵗ morning report.

5. Casualty returns reports will be made by each section from 8am. to 8am. and must be sent to arrive daily at advanced Coy H.Q. by 7am at latest.

6. **Guides.** A guide will meet the sections at 7ᵗʰ M.G.C. H.Q. at GORRE at 3.15 pm. and team guides will be at advanced Coy H.Q. at 4 p.m.

7. Sections will march at 200 yards distance from TUNING FORK ROAD to advanced Coy. H.Q.

8. Rations will be sent daily to advanced Coy. H.Q. and will be drawn at dawn each morning.

9. Acknowledge

Copy No 1 7ᵗʰ Bgde.
     2 7ᵗʰ M.G.Coy
     3 Lᵗ Brutton
     4 2/Lᵗ Hind
     5   "   Wilkins
     6   War Diary

W.W. Ashcroft Capt
Comᵈ 195 MGC

BEUVRY
21/10/17. 9.30. am.

Headquarters　　　　　　　　110/A/17
110 Inf. Brigade　　　　　　　26-7-16

Narrative of Work of 110 M.G. Coy
from 3am July 14th to 8 am July 17th

14-7-16
3am The Company at this hour was
disposed as follows:-
No 2 & No 3 Sections occupied WOOD
TRENCH
No 1 & No 4 Sections were at this time
in QUADRANGLE SUPPORT trench
No 4 Section under 2/Lieut Bramer
being under orders to move forward
& help consolidate the infantry
objective
Orders were received & forwarded to
O.C. No 4 Section to move forward
to the N. edge of BAZENTIN WOOD
About 5.30 am 2/Lieut BRAMER
having become a casualty the
Section moved forward under
2/Lieut JOSEPH
No 2 Section were then ordered to
move forward & occupy the position
vacated by No 4 Section

2

At 8 am No 2 Section under Lieut- CROWDY were ordered to take up a position in MAMETZ WOOD along the N edge to cover the left edge of BAZENTIN WOOD in case of a enemy counter attack.

By 10.35 am 2/Lieut JOSEPH with four guns had reached the front edge of the wood & had the guns in position as follows:-

Two guns about 250 yds from the N.W corner & two guns at the N.E corner W of the main road through BAZENTIN-LE-PETIT village & enfilading the N edge of the wood.

The enemy counter attacked & were taken in enfilade by the two guns in the N.E corner & were badly damaged by our fire.

At this time ammunition was beginning to be a difficult question & these two guns ran out of it & had to temporarily withdraw to the support line in the wood. This was due to the fact that heavy guns had also been short. None of our carrying parties was detailed to supply them & time was lost in getting a further carrying party from the Brigade

3

Throughout the whole of the operations great difficulty was experienced in supplying guns with water & ammunition. Carrying parties had been allotted for this purpose but were not of the best type available. Ammunition carrying is a job requiring physical qualities & resource & except for two or three men these qualities were most conspicuous by their absence in the majority of carrying parties.

The officer i/c of No 4 Section having retired where two guns left there under an N.C.O with orders to await his return. After waiting 2 to 3 hours this N.C.O having had one gun damaged, withdrew into MAMETZ WOOD & reported to the O C Coy at Bn H.Qrs that the officer in question was missing. The time was now about 9.30pm — about 10.0pm 2/Lieut ANDERSON was ordered to take his section (No 3) forward to occupy a position along the N edge of BAZENTIN WOOD. The guide who was sent with No 3 Section lost his way &

left the party was the N W corner which was not entirely cleared of the enemy. S/Sergt ANDERSON became a casualty & gave orders to his sergeant to withdraw the section & report to Coy HQ.

At ..... on the 15th inst No 3 Section went forward again under an officer & were disposed as follows:
Two guns occupied a siding garrisoned by the R.I. in the N E corner, one gun in the trench occupied by own infantry toe in an emplacement on the N edge constructed by a pioneer company. During the night 15/16 a weak counter attack was delivered by the enemy which was easily repulsed.

Early on the morning of the 16th the remaining gun of No 4 Section was sent forward & took up a position on the left edge of the wood to enfilade an enemy CT which was being used for the advance of enemy bombers. This trench was successfully enfiladed.

The Company was relieved on the

evening of the 16th by the 61st
M G Coy the relief was
successfully completed the Coy
moved to bivouacs for the night
in a field S E of FRICOURT WOOD
at X 4 a.

During the time No 2 Section were
in position on the N edge of
MAMETZ WOOD a considerable
number of "new type gas" shells
were sent over.

The new box respirator was used
& proved perfectly satisfactory
protection against the gas

The following N.C.Os. & men have
been recommended for particularly
good work during the operations
  Sergt WOODROW
    "   BARTLETT
    "   BROWN
  Pte GOODRIDGE
    "   RIDLEY

Subject: Battle of the SOMME. July 1916

No 2 Section 110th M.G. Coy

On Monday 10th July, my section moved up with the Company from MERICOURT via MÉAULTE to FRICOURT arriving there about 10pm. I was ordered to take my section up to the then front line trench viz QUADRANGLE TRENCH to relieve two guns of the 62nd M.G Coy there, & to place my other two guns in reserve. On the way up our guide lost his way and we ran into some extremely heavy shelling near BOTTOM WOOD. The section however luckily escaped any casualties and arrived & carried out the relief about 2 am having taken 3 hours en route. We then found that an attack was in progress on the trench in front viz QUADRANGLE SUPPORT, but it was not until daylight that we learned that it was entirely successful. At about 6 am I was joined by Mr GORDON who had been sent up to assist me.

Tuesday July 11th.
During the day the section remained in QUADRANGLE TRENCH until I had reconnoitred the new front line for

positions. This was by no means an easy thing to do, as the shelling was incessant during the whole day. During the day I laid one gun to fire indirectly on BAZENTIN WOOD & another from QUADRANGLE SUPPORT trench firing at BAZENTIN VILLAGE. As soon as it was dusk, I moved another gun up into QUADRANGLE SUPPORT trench (left flank) now having two here & two in support in QUADRANGLE TRENCH in charge of Mr GORDON. Shelling continued intermittently throughout the night.

Wednesday July 12th

Early in the morning at "Stand to" an intensive bombardment took place, lasting about ½ an hour. Nothing further happened. One gun emplacement in QUADRANGLE SUPPORT trench was hit & gun steam buried. Little harm was done to either. Little doing during the day. Intermittent shelling behind our front of the trench. Carried on indirect fire as before mentioned. One casualty in QUADRANGLE trench. We "stood to" from 10 am to 1.30 pm. At "stand to" in the evening we were treated to another short & sharp bombardment — several shells landing on parados & dug outs, burying some

men including my gunners on one
occasion. At 10pm the two guns in
QUADRANGLE TRENCH were relieved, &
the other two in QUADRANGLE SUPPORT
about 1.am on

Thursday July 13th
when we returned to FRICOURT for a
brief rest.
At 6pm I went up to WOOD TRENCH to lay
out lines for indirect fire on various points
in BAZENTIN WOOD. This was successfully
achieved & the guns were then brought
up by Mr Gordon & opened fire from 11.15 pm
to 12 midnight - firing between 4000 & 5000
rounds in all. I then placed the men
in the trench (after dismounting guns)
& awaited further orders. At 6am on

Friday July 14th
I received orders to move my section forward
to Bn Hd Qrs on edge of MAMETZ WOOD
At about 8am I was told to move up
to the front of MAMETZ WOOD & take up
positions covering the left of BAZENTIN
WOOD in case of German counterattack
- most of this wood was now in our hands
Heavy shelling of MAMETZ WOOD & the
ground to the left was in progress
but aided by extraordinarily good fortune

I managed to get men & guns up safely to a sheltered position - of a kind - under a bank - without casualties. I then with a scout went forward to reconnoitre. On our way back we were both blown up by a large shell but unharmed. I then got the guns into position. We experienced considerable discomfort from lachrymatory & gas shells at this period. Having placed my guns we then got in touch with troops on our right & left & later with the men holding BAZENTIN WOOD to our front.
We remained here during the day & the day following.

Saturday July 15th when Mr GORDON left me taking

Sunday July 16th without seeing any good targets or receiving any orders to move up further. I received very little information as to the progress of events elsewhere. At 7.30pm I received orders to evacuate my positions & move back to Bat Hd Qts. During this period I had one man killed & three temporarily out of action from shell shock. Heavy shelling went on in in front of behind us, especially with gas shells, but respirators (box pattern) proved entirely satisfactory against the effects of these.

One gun was very nearly knocked out by a shell which pitched about 6 feet in front of the position.

We got back to bivouac near MAMETZ without mishap. Throughout the whole period

July 10th – 16th

great difficulty was experienced with regard to carrying of ammunition water etc – owing to shortage of men. All my men behaved with the greatest calmness and difficulty was too great for them to overcome with cheerfulness under the most trying circumstances. N.C.Os especially deserve great praise.

(Sd). Ronald St J Crowdy – Lieut
1/c No 2 Section
110 M.G. Coy.

In the Field
28th July 1916

Subject:- Battle of the SOMME. July 1916
No 4 Section 110th M.G. Coy.

Sir,

I have the honour to make the following report of operations in the fighting in BAZENTIN-LE-PETIT wood & village on July 14th 15th & 16th last.

Early on the morning of 14th July (Mr BRAMER being wounded) I advanced with No 4 Section into BAZENTIN LE PETIT wood. Heavy shell fire was experienced between MAMETZ WOOD & BAZENTIN WOOD. I established a subsection (two guns) at a point about 250 yds from the N.W. corner of the wood. Our line ran along the left edge of the wood & did not include the whole of the N.W. corner.

I crossed the wood & established the remaining subsection at the N.E corner of the wood. W of the main road of BAZENTIN LE PETIT village. An enemy counterattack took place almost immediately. Both guns did valuable work in repelling this counterattack.

I advanced one gun in front of the village & this gun proved particularly useful. Sgt. WOODROW was wounded whilst firing this gun. This subsection ran out of ammunition & I withdrew the two guns to a support line in BAZENTIN WOOD & awaited the arrival of a further supply. In the meantime leaving my only remaining N.C.O. in charge I visited Bn H.Qrs of the Infantry to discuss the situation & the best possible dispositions of my guns. This support line was subjected to heavy shelling for two hours & the N.C.O referred to above (Cpl SONGER) withdrew the guns one of which had been damaged to MAMETZ WOOD. The ammunition supply had now arrived & accordingly I dumped the 20 boxes near Bn H.Qrs of the 9th LEICESTERS

No 3 Section was now sent up from MAMETZ WOOD — Cpl SONGER acting as guide. It was by this time quite dark the O.C. No 3 Section was wounded & the guide was cut off. Accordingly No 3 Section Sergeant returned to Bat H.Qrs with the section.

At about 8am on Saturday 15th I took No 3 Section into BAZENTIN WOOD

collected the 20 boxes I had dumped
& established one subsection in the
N.E corner of wood in a strong point
erected by the R.E's. I established
the other two guns as follows:-
One in our trench running along left
edge of wood - this by arrangement
with O.C 8th Bn LEICESTER REGT &
one gun actually in the edge of the
wood in an emplacement I had had
made by a Pioneer Company. This gun
had a particularly good field of fire.
By this time ammunition supply
water supply, the carrying of
messages were running smoothly -
the carrying party attached however
were a source of much trouble &
inconvenience. Several were lost
some I believe rejoined their
companies on the journey between
Bde HQ & myself
During the night 15/16 July the enemy
attempted a weak counterattack
which was easily repulsed.
Snipers were very troublesome but
at least two were accounted for
On Sunday 16th we were free from
their attention.

Early on the morning of the 16th July I took over the remaining teams & gun of No 4 Section who had with me a total of seven guns. This gun I placed in a suitable position on the left edge of the wood to deal with an enemy communication trench which was being constantly used by their bombing parties. This trench was successfully enfiladed.

I was relieved in the evening of the 16th by S.P.Y. The relief was carried out without any hitch.

(sd) M. Joseph 2nd Lieut

110th M.G. Coy

WAR DIARY.

INTELLIGENCE SUMMARY.

(Erase heading not required.)

Place	Date	Hour	Summary of Events and Information	Remarks and references to Appendices
HUMBERCAMPS	July 1		Under orders for movements tonight	
"	2		DITTO	
"	3	9am	moved to billets in LA BAZEQUE FARM	
LA BAZEQUE	5		Training	
"	6	2pm	Refs billets. at 2 pm 2 marches to TALMAS via PAS - MARIEUX - DOCHEVILLERS - Company billeted for night	
TALMAS	7	6.30am	left TALMAS marched to LE QUESNOIT FARM near CROUY via VIGNA COURT - HANGEST=CROUX - arriving by 3 pm Good billets for men	
LE QUESNOIT	8		men resting	
"	9		men resting	
"	10	2am	Company moved by motor route to AILLE-SUR-SOMME arrivance at 10am for MERICOURT - detrained at 2 pm moved by lorries to MEAULTE arriving 3.30 pm Bivouacked in field the evening	

INTELLIGENCE SUMMARY.

(Erase heading not required.)

Summaries are contained in F. S. Regs., Part II. and the Staff Manual respectively. Title pages will be prepared in manuscript.

Place	Date	Hour	Summary of Events and Information	Remarks and references to Appendices
	July			
MEAULTE	10	8.30pm	Headqrs. marched to FRICOURT, right over H.Q. from No. 5.5 M. G. Coy relieves two sections in front support also two sections in reserve at FRICOURT.	X
FRICOURT	10	11pm	No. 2 Section under Lieut CROWDY and 3 Sections under 2/Lt ANDERSON went forward to relieve corresponding sections of 64th M.G. Coy in QUADRANGLE TRENCH. The relief was completed by 5 am. Guns were being brought up in progress. Heavy enemy bombardment being in progress.	X
,,	11		No. 2 Section moved forward into QUADRANGLE SUPPORT trench.	X
,,	11	2pm	2/Lt G.E. BOWMAN wounded in the head with shrapnel.	X X
,,	12	10pm	Relief of 2+3 Sections by 64th M.G. Coy commences & successfully completion by 5 am 13th inst.	X
,,	13	5am	Relief of 2+3 Sections complete	X
,,	13	9pm	Coy HQ & no moved forward to 98th Inf gps in MAMETZ WOOD & dispositions for the attack on BAZENTIN-LE-PETIT WOOD were prepared.	X

INTELLIGENCE SUMMARY.

(Erase heading not required.)

Summaries are contained in F. S. Regs., Part II. and the Staff Manual respectively. Title pages will be prepared in manuscript.

Place	Date	Hour	Summary of Events and Information	Remarks and references to Appendices
MAMETZ WOOD	14		No details of action are apparent. A.B. & C. attached given narratives of Coy. work during the period take a personal	&
" "	15		Account written by OC 4 + OC 2 Section	&
" "	16	6pm	Relieved by 6/7 M.G. Coy moved down to transport lines officer completion of relief – arriving Bivouacs at 10am. 1st Lieut. injured	&
BUY			Total casualties 5 officers wounded OR 3 killed 134 wounded	&
FRICOURT	17		Stayed in Bivouac till evening. Enemy shelled valley	
WOOD			intermittently throughout day. No casualties	&
LITZ		8am	moved by march route back to RIBEMONT nr MAULTE	&
			DERNANCOURT. Billeted in sugar factory	
RIBEMONT	18		Company resting & cleaning guns etc.	&
	19		Inspection by G.O.C. 21st Division	&
	20		Marched to MERICOURT entrained at 10am for SALEUX arrived SALEUX 2pm. detrained marched to LE QUESNOIT	&
			FARM arriving 4.45 pm	
LE QUESNOIT	21		Received orders to move by main bus to LONGPRE at 5pm	&

INTELLIGENCE SUMMARY.
(Erase heading not required.)

Summaries are contained in F.S. Regs, Part II. and the Staff Manual respectively. Title pages will be prepared in manuscript.

Place	Date	Hour	Summary of Events and Information	Remarks and references to Appendices
	21		Horses arrived here at 12 P.M. arrived LONGPRE at 1.30 am & bivouacked in transport lines	S.
	22	9.40am	Marched from LONGPRE to LONGEAU nr AMIENS & entrained for HOUVIN leaving at 12.45 pm	
		5 pm	Arrived HOUVIN detrained marched to billets in GOUY-en-TERNOIS	S.
GOUY	23		Cleaning guns etc	S.
"	24	7.30pm	Received orders to move to billets at LATTRE ST QUENTIN horses & men were conveyed in our billets which were very poor	S.
LATTRE	25		Resting Refitting. Two staff officers reported for duty	
ST QUENTIN	26		This section under the O.C. moved by lorry to SANEVILLE 1	
"	27	10.30am	Proceeded from there by march route to ARRAS to relieve the 43rd Fd. Q. Coy. Relief completed by 2.30 am 26th mar. Company deposed as follows 1 & 2 sections in the line 3 section in reserve one Reserve at Company Headquarters nr	

INTELLIGENCE SUMMARY.
(Erase heading not required.)

Summaries are contained in F.S. Regs., Part II.
and the Staff Manual respectively. Title pages
will be prepared in manuscript.

Place	Date	Hour	Summary of Events and Information	Remarks and references to Appendices
ARRAS	28		ARRAS. 4 Section in Wanbrin part in Wanbrin Situation quiet	J. S. XXX
"	29		" " " "	
"	30		" " " "	
"	31		" " " "	

110th Brigade.

21st Division.

110th BRIGADE MACHINE GUN COMPANY

AUGUST 1916

Army Form C. 2118.

WAR DIARY
or
INTELLIGENCE SUMMARY.
(Erase heading not required.)

Instructions regarding War Diaries and Intelligence Summaries are contained in F. S. Regs., Part II. and the Staff Manual respectively. Title pages will be prepared in manuscript.

N⁰ 110 M. GUN COMPANY.

Place	Date	Hour	Summary of Events and Information	Remarks and references to Appendices
	1916 August			
ARRAS	1		Nos. 1 & 2 Sections (8 guns) in the line, Nos 3 & 4 Sections in Brigade and Divisional reserve in ARRAS & WARLUS respectively. Front held in front of ST NICOLAS Station quiet	e
	2		ditto	e
	3		ditto	e
	4		ditto	e
	5		No 4 Section moved up from WARLUS to ARRAS. Lt W. & FANNING took over command of No 4 Section and relieved No 2 Section. 2/Lt G.B. WHEELER took over command of No 3 Section. Relieved No 1 Section. Nos 1 & 2 sections moved back into billets in ARRAS. Relief complete by 8.30 pm	See appendix "A"
	6		Station normal except some hostile artillery activity during night 5-6th August	e
	7		ditto	e
	8		ditto	e

Army Form C. 2118.

WAR DIARY
or
INTELLIGENCE SUMMARY.
(Erase heading not required.)

Instructions regarding War Diaries and Intelligence Summaries are contained in F. S. Regs., Part II. and the Staff Manual respectively. Title pages will be prepared in manuscript.

Place	Date	Hour	Summary of Events and Information	Remarks and references to Appendices
ARRAS	1916 August			
	9		Situation quiet	8/c
	10		ditto. 2/Lt FOSTER R.S. reported for duty	8/e
	11		ditto.	8/e
	12		ditto.	8/e
	13		ditto. Nos 1 & 2 sections relieved nos 3 & 4 sections in the line. Nos 3 & 4 sections returned to billets in ARRAS	8/e 8/c
	14		ditto. 2/Lt K. GORDON & 2/Lt A.G. BUTCHER reported for duty.	8/e 8/c
	15		ditto.	8/e 8/c
	16		ditto.	8/c
	17		ditto. Re-adjustment of Company front. No 1 Section returned to billets in ARRAS. Nos 3 & 4 section moved up into the line. No 2 section remained in the line. Four gun positions taken over from No 62 M.G. Coy by No 3 Section. One subsection of No 1 took over two guns from No 62 M.G. Coy., South of the SCARPE	

Army Form C. 2118.

WAR DIARY
or
INTELLIGENCE SUMMARY.
(Erase heading not required.)

Instructions regarding War Diaries and Intelligence Summaries are contained in F. S. Regs., Part II. and the Staff Manual respectively. Title pages will be prepared in manuscript.

Place	Date	Hour	Summary of Events and Information	Remarks and references to Appendices
	1916 August			
ARRAS	17(cont)		The three subsections of No.4 took over two guns from No.1 Section	See appendix "B"
	18		No.1 Section evacuated two gun positions in OBSERVATORY REDOUBT.	
			Sr. Section quiet	
	19		ditto	
	20		ditto	
	21		ditto	
	22		ditto / 2 Guns of No.3 Section relieved by 2 guns M.M.G. Battery. (Aug 23")	
	23		ditto. Indirect fire carried out all night on front G.18 & G.2 & vicinity.	
	24		ditto. No.2 Section in the line relieved by No.1 Section No.2 Section returned to Billets in ARRAS.	See appendix "c"
	25		ditto	
	26		ditto	
	27		ditto	
	28		ditto	
	29		ditto	

Army Form C. 2118.

WAR DIARY
or
INTELLIGENCE SUMMARY.

Place	Date	Hour	Summary of Events and Information	Remarks and references to Appendices
ARRAS	1916 August 30.		No 2 Section relieved two guns of No 3 Section + 2 guns of M.M.G.	See appendix "D" 8/c
	31		Situation quiet	

Operation Order No 1
by Capt A.B. Bowden
Commdg 110 M.G. Coy

1/ 1 & 2 Sections will be relieved by 3 & 4 Sections on the night of 5/6 August.

2/ Lieut W.G. Fanning will command No 4 Section & will relieve No 2 Section. 2/Lt G.B. Wheeler will command No 3 Section & will relieve No 1 Section.

3/ OC 1 & 2 Sections will arrange for a guide from each gun team to be at Coy H.Q 2nd by 5.45 pm 5th inst.

4/ Relieving sections will take over tripods – ammunition boxes & all trench stores & duplicate receipts will be given – one copy being retained & one copy handed to this office.
Guns & spare parts will NOT be handed over.

5/ Reports to Coy HQ 2nd by Section Officers on completion of relief.

6/ Nos 1 & 2 Sections will move back into billets in ARRAS. No 1 Section will be in Divisional reserve & No 2 Section in Bde reserve

7. Relieving sections will move off from Coy HQs 2nd in following order.

RIGHT SECTOR
No 3 Section
J2-1 & J2-2 guns 6.30pm.
BRITTANIA WORKS }
NICHOLLS REDOUBT } 6.45 pm

LEFT SECTOR.
No 4 Section.
Two observatory guns 6.0 pm
DOSKY & NOVEMBER guns 6.15 pm.

A H Bowden Capt.
OC 110 M & Coy.

SECRET

No.11 Machine Gun Coy   Copy No. 10
  Operation Order No 5A

1. The 11th M.G. Coy will adjust [dispositions]
& dispositions in the course of 17/18
August 1916.

2. For the purpose of administration the
Company frontage will be divided into
3 Sectors viz LEFT. CENTRE. RIGHT
The LEFT Sector will be manned by
No 2 Section less one gun, plus one
subsection of No 4 will be under
the command of LIEUT. CROWDY.
The CENTRE Sector will be manned
by No 3 Section plus one gun of No 4
Section & will be commanded by
2nd LIEUT. WHEELER.
The RIGHT Sector will be manned by
one subsection of No 4 Section & will
be commanded by LIEUT. FANNING.

3. Reliefs will be carried out as under
           LEFT SECTOR
One subsection of No 4 Section will
relieve the two guns of No 1 Section
at present occupying BOSKY and
NOVEMBER emplacements. OBSERVATORY
& SUNDAY AVENUE positions will be

vaseline & all section equipment for these two guns returned to Coy HQ 2nd
Trench Stores will be handed over to a representative from Bn M.G. Coy & duplicates obtained
The two guns of No 4 Section relieving BOSKY 1 NOVEMBER will leave Coy HQ 2nd at 2.30pm.
On completion of relief OC No 1 Section will proceed with his section to Coy HQ 2nd in ARRAS where the Section will be held in Brig.ade reserve
No 2 Section will remain as at present except that the gun now occupying J1 will be moved into the MACHINE GUN REDOUBT - the gun team will take over the position & dug out now held by OR OR M.G. Coy. This transfer will commence at 2.30pm
The same night lines as for J1 gun with a slightly increased range will be the direction of fire for this gun
OC No 2 Section will make all necessary arrangements for this Transfer. Map Reference M.G Redoubt: 51b NW3. G.12 c.05.65 approx.

CENTRE SECTOR

No 3 Section will take over the following emplacements now occupied by 62 MG Coy:-
J1 - J2 - APRIL and MAY.

Guides for the above guns will be at 110th Bgd's S/D R'd at 5 pm

O.C no 3 Section will report to Coy H.Q R'd at 11 am tomorrow to receive instructions as to lines of fire as the existing lines now used by 62 M G Coy will not be the same in all cases.

All trench stores will be taken over & duplicate receipts obtained

RIGHT SECTOR

The remaining subsection of N2 4 Section will receive the following emplacements now held by 62 M.G Coy.

IVORY ROAD & INNS OF COURT

Guides for above guns will be at Coy S/D 2nd at 6 pm.

Trench stores will be taken over & duplicate receipts obtained

2 copies of receipts for all trench stores taken over will be forwarded to Coy S/D R'd by 4 pm the 18th inst. These returns must also show particulars of all S.A.A Grenades, Very lights etc taken over

5. Where guns are relieving their own Company guns, Section equipment with the exception of guns spare parts will be handed over – where guns of 62 M G Coy are being relieved NO section equipment will be handed over.

6. Completion of relief to be reported to Coy HQ R[?] by wiring the word BUTCHER.

7. Acknowledge please.

Issued at 10.30 pm 16-8-16 18
Copy No 1   OC 62 M G Coy.
         2   Transport Officer
         3   OC No 1 Section
         4   OC No 2 Section
         5   OC No 3 Section
         6   OC No 4 Section
         7   Office Copy
        8 & 9   War Diary
        10   OC 64 M G Coy

A.H. Bowden Capt
Commdg 110 M G Coy

SECRET.   COPY

Operation Order No 3 A

1. No 2 Section will be relieved by
No 1 Section on the night of 24th Aug 1916

2. Guides from No 2 Section will be at
Coy H.Q. H.Q. at 5.30 pm on the 24th

3. Trench stores bombs &c will be
handed over to relieving section
Guns & spare parts will NOT be
handed over.

4. Duplicate receipts for all stores
taken over will be given — one
copy to reach this office by
4 pm 25th inst.

5. Completion of relief will be reported
by wiring the word "GONE" to Coy
H.Q. 2.B.

A.H. Borden Capt. O.C.
No 110 M. GUN COMPANY.

Issued at 6 pm 23.8.16 - PB

Copy No 1 OC No 1 Section
        2 OC No 2   "
        3 OC No 3   "
        4 OC No 4   "
        5 Office
        6 War Diary

SECRET. (App D) Copy No.

Operation Order No 4.

1. Two guns of No 3 Section & two guns of Motor Machine Gun Batty will be relieved by No 2 Section on the night of 30th August.
2. Guides from No 3 Section & the M.M.G. Batty will be at Coy H.Q. 2nd By 5.30 pm
3. Trench Stores - tripods etc will be handed over to relieving section. Guns & spare parts will NOT be handed over
4. Duplicate receipts for all trench stores taken over will be given - one copy to reach this office by 4 pm 31st inst.
5. Completion of relief will be reported by wiring the word "SILVER" to Coy H.Q. 2nd. Acknowledge

Issued at to.
Copy No 1 OC No 1 Section
 " 2 OC No 2 Section
 3 OC No 3 Section
 4 OC No 4 Section
 5 Office
 6, 7 War Diary

Barrott
No 110 M. GUN COMPANY

110th Brigade.
21st Division.

110th BRIGADE MACHINE GUN COMPANY

SEPTEMBER 1916.

Army Form C. 2118.

WAR DIARY
or
INTELLIGENCE SUMMARY.
(Erase heading not required.)

Instructions regarding War Diaries and Intelligence Summaries are contained in F. S. Regs., Part II. and the Staff Manual respectively. Title pages will be prepared in manuscript.

Place	Date	Hour	Summary of Events and Information	Remarks and references to Appendices
ARRAS	Aug 1st 1916		Goostown in Reserve situation normal.	
"	2		do	
"	3		Company was relieved by Pte 10th Machine Gun Coy. Operation orders for this move are attached as appendix "A"	
MONTENESCOURT	4	10am	Arrived in billets in this village	
"	4	9am	Coy. Montenescourt marched to billets in Berneaucourt arriving 2.30 p.m.	
BERNEACOURT	5th 10th 12th		Training during this period.	
"	13		Coy. Berneacourt at 2.30 p.m. and marched to Frevent 15 arriving per Heilly.	
FREVENT	14	6am	Entrained & moved off at this hour.	
HEILLY	14	9am	D'trained marched to about D18c Ref. 4/40000 Albert Sheet 8	
"	15		Coy. D18c marched to Bernaecourt arriving about 10am.	
BERNAECOURT	15	2.30pm	Coy. Bernaecourt marched to Fricourt Camp. Where it commenced.	

Army Form C. 2118.

WAR DIARY
or
INTELLIGENCE SUMMARY.
(Erase heading not required.)

Instructions regarding War Diaries and Intelligence Summaries are contained in F. S. Regs., Part II. and the Staff Manual respectively. Title pages will be prepared in manuscript.

Place	Date	Hour	Summary of Events and Information	Remarks and references to Appendices
	1916			
FRICOURT	16	9.30pm	Marched off at 9.30pm assembled at POMMIERS REDOUBT arrived at 12am. Three 10 minute halts en bivouacs for this march.	X
CAMP			Two Sections marched off at 9am to MONTAUBAN arrived	X
POMMIERS REDOUBT	17	9am	at 10am to take over defence of village.	X
	18	4pm	The remainder Two sections arrived MONTAUBAN 10 prepare for the attack.	X
MONTAUBAN	19, 10, 21, 22, 23.		Under orders to proceed forward to attack GUEUDECOURT	X
MONTAUBAN	24	4pm	No 4 Section moved forward to relieve four guns of M.G. Coy in Butt Rd Trench.	X
	25	11.30am	Remainder of company moved forward to take up position prior to attack. Operation orders for this move are attached as appendix "B".	X
	26 to 30		Conference with Balkan division. This forward movement of divisions attacked as appendix "C"	X

APPENDIX "A" Copy No 8.

Operation order No 4A.

1. The 110th M.G. Coy will be relieved by the 105 M.G. Coy on Sept 3rd 1916.
On completion of relief, sections will be marched back to Coy Headquarters in ARRAS.

2/. Guides from each gun will be at Coy. HQrs at 8.30 A.M on the 3rd inst. to guide relieving guns in.

3/ All trench stores will be handed over & the forms already in possession of section officers will be countersigned by the relieving officer of the 105th M.G. Coy. Trench maps will be counted as trench stores & handed over accordingly.

4 Lieut W. G. FANNING with a billeting party of two men will report to the Town Major of BERLENCOURT at 10.30 am on the 4th inst.

2

4. To take over Company billets.
5. Relief of all guns is to be complete by 12.30 p.m. 3rd inst.
6. On the 4th Sept. the Company will move into rest billets at BERLENCOURT & will move off at 9.30 a.m. on that date.
7. Officers Valises to be at Coy. Hqrs by 2-0 am on the 3rd inst, ready to load on to transport.

Symbol 1 - O.C. 1 Sec
       2   2 —
       3   3 —
       4   4 —
       5   T.O. —
       6   10's in Coy.
       7   Officers Coy.
       8/9   W – Signals

APPENDIX "B"

SECRET.   COPY NO 6

Operation Orders no 5
by Capt A G Bowden
Comndg 110 ~~Inf Bde~~ M G Coy

1. The 110 Inf Bde will relieve the 15th Durham L.I. (64 Inf Bde) & take up a position of assembly during the night of 24/25 Sept 1916.

2. Bde boundaries are as shown on maps already issued. The boundaries between the 8th & 9th Bns Leicester Regts will be approx T1d 25.60 – N31d 98.65 – N32a 33.25

3. One Section of the 110 M G Coy will relieve one Section of 64 M G Coy in BULL RD Trench. Relief to be carried out under arrangements of OCs concerned. One guide from 64 M G Coy to meet No 4 Section at 64 M G Coy HQrs 2nd at 7 pm. The two sections 110 M G Coy detailed to work with 8th & 9th Leicester Regts will move to RAP Trench. To be in position by daylight. Remaining Section will be in reserve about S6d 6.3.

4. Trench emplacements will be improved as far as possible during hours of darkness.

5. During night of 24/25 BOAT & GIRD trenches will be frequently swept by M.G. fire. O.C. No 4 Section to make necessary arrangements to prevent the enemy working on the wire.

6. Until ZERO on the 25 inst there must be as little movement as possible in order that the enemy may not know that the trenches are held more strongly than usual & that new trenches are occupied.

7. Completion of relief & arrival in assembly position will be reported to Coy HQ 2nds immediately.

8. Battalion & Bde HQrs 2nds will be as follows
8 & 9 Bn Leicesters combined HQ 2nds about T1.b.50.45.
6th Bn Leic Regt in SWITCH trench about T1.d.1.8.
7th Bn Leic Regt near junction on BROWN trench & COCOA LANE
Bde HQ 2nds S.b.85.15.

9. Acknowledge Please

A H Bowden, Capt
OC 110 M.G. Coy

Issued at 2.30pm 24 Sept 1916 W

Copy No 1   OC No 1 Section
       2   2
       3   3
       4   4
       5   Transport Officer
     6+7   War Diary
       8   Office
       9   OC 64 M G Coy

APPENDIX "C"

Synopsis of operations of 110 Machine Gun Company from 6 pm 24.9.16 to midnight 1/2 Oct.

1. At midnight on 24.9.16 the Company moved from MONTAUBAN to take up positions prior to the attack. On completion of relief of 64th Machine Gun Company the Company was situated as follows:—

No 1 Section in reserve at Brigade Headquarters

No 2 Section in GAP TRENCH with 'B' Company of 9th Batt. Leicestershire Regt.

No 3 Section in GAP TRENCH with Company of 8th Batt. Leicestershire Regt.

No 4 Section in BULL ROAD TRENCH which at this period was our front line, from dawn on the 25th September to the hour of the attack this section engaged several targets in front of GUEUDECOURT village and five hostile aeroplanes.

2. Previous to the attack orders were issued from Coy H.Qrs as follows. No 1 Section to remain in reserve at BDE H.Qrs.

No 2 Section to advance with the rear Company of 9th Batt Leicestershire Regt and consolidate right half of Brigade front on

2

reaching objective.

No 3 Section to advance with the rear Company of 8th Batt. Leicestershire Reg't and consolidate left half of Brigade front on reaching final objective.

No 4 Section to remain in BULL ROAD trench during the attack and be prepared to move forward to GIRD TRENCH as local reserve to Nos 2 and 3 Sections on receiving orders from Coy Hd Qrs

3. Administration of Sections prior to attack.
Forty men were attached to the Company from 7th Batt. Leicestershire Reg't as carrying party and were distributed as follows:-

No 1 Section 5 men   No 2 Section 15 men
No 3 Section 15 men   No 4 Section 5 men

The strength of each Section exclusive of carrying party previous to the attack was 22 O.R including N.C.O's and Officers Servants

The section equipment was carried into action as follows:-

No 1 & 4 Sections (In reserve) and Front line

S.A.A

The numbers one, two and three of each gun team carried between them Gun Tripod and two belt boxes per gun.

3

	S.A.A
= 8 boxes per section.	2,000 rds
The two Officers Servants carried two extra belts not in boxes =	1,000
Remainder of section (8 men) 3 belt boxes each	6,000
Attached men 5	
2 Carried two petrol cans of water each. = 4 Petrol cans of Water	
3 Carried 3 belt boxes each	2,250
Officers 2 Carried six bandoliers each	600
Total S.A.A	11,850

Nos 2 and 3 Sections (attacking)
The numbers one two and three of each gun team carried between them Gun Tripod and two belt boxes per gun — 2,000
Two Officers Servants carried two belts not in boxes — 1,000
Remainder of section (8 men) 3 boxes each — 6,000
Attached men (15)
4 Carried 3 boxes (belt) each — 5,250
3 carried 2 belt boxes and 1 water carrier each — 1,500
3 carried 6 Petrol Cans of Water
2 Carried 15 bandoliers each — 1,500
Officers (2) Carried six bandoliers each — 600

Total S.A.A — 14,850

4

Three empty sandbags were carried by every man and found exceedingly useful during consolidation.

The canvas water carriers were not found to be a success as they very soon leaked.

4. At ZERO the 25th Sept the infantry advanced and at 12.45 No 2 Section arrived at the SUNKEN ROAD which formed the right boundary of the attack. This Section advanced towards GIRD TRENCH but found the attack held up by machine gun fire and fell back to BULL ROAD TRENCH. ~~but found~~ and established four guns with B Coy of the 9th Batt. Leicestershire Regt.

No 3 Section had also advanced with Coy of 8th Batt. Leicestershire Regt and were now established in BULL ROAD TRENCH.

At this period Nos 2, 3 and 4 Sections were in BULL ROAD TRENCH.

At 6 pm on 26th September No 4 Section and No 3 Section received orders from Coy No 2 to advance with 6th Batt. Leicestershire Regiment into GUEUDECOURT VILLAGE. No 4 Section to establish themselves on the right half of the village and No 3 on the left. No 2 were ordered to establish themselves in GIRD TRENCH having

5

had heavy casualties. A heavy barrage on the sunken road at N 26 d 50.40 compelled O.C. No 4 Section to temporarily establish his guns in GIRD SUPPORT. Darkness then set in and at 5.30 am No 4 Section had taken up the following positions on the outskirts of GUEUDECOURT VILLAGE. Two guns on left of main road at N. 26 b 90.90 and N 26 b 10.85 respectively. Two guns on right of main road at N 27 a. 10.60 and N 27. a 15.50 respectively. A carrying party lent by O.C. 6th Batt. Leicestershire Regt enabled this section to take over from No 2. Section the extra ammunition and water previously detailed to be carried by the attacking Sections.

At 11.30 am on 27th September No 3 Section had advanced into GUEUDECOURT and were ordered to take up a position on left edge of the village to support the attack of the 55th Division. The remaining two guns of No 3 Section took over the two position held by No 4 Section on the left of the main road thus enabling No 4 Section to concentrate on the defence of the right half of the village by placing these two guns at N 27. a. 10.45. and N. 27a. 20.35. The two guns of No 3 Section covering the advance

6

of the 55th Division on our left were situated at N.266.60.75 approximately.

The remainder of the day 27th and the next few days (viz. 28th 29th & 30th Sept) were spent in the improvement and strengthening of gun positions.

Many excellent targets were engaged by all guns and effectively disposed of. One sniper who had done much execution was killed on the morning of the 29th Sept. The guns were firing at ranges varying from 400 to 1000 yards continually at parties of the enemy recklessly exposing himself.

One complete gun team was sent to O.C. No 2 Section as reinforcements and 6 men to No 3 Section and 6 men to No 4 Section this washed out the personnel of the Section in reserve at Bn H.Q 2ns. Application was then made to Bde H.Q. for reinforcements and five gun teams from 64th M.G. Coy arrived at 7.0 pm on Sept 29th.

Four of these gun teams were sent to man the four guns in GIRD TRENCH which at this time only one could have been used sentries being posted on the remaining three.

A marked improvement was noticeable in the personnel of the attached men and no trouble was experienced at any time during the operations with the supply of ammunition and water. The Company was relieved on the evening of Oct 1st by 37th Machine Gun Company, which relief was successfully carried out by handing over to the relieving Company Belt boxes and Tripods. The Company then moved to MONTAUBAN. The casualties in the Company during the first 36 hours after ZERO were as follows:-

    2 Officers wounded
    5 O.R. killed
    34 O.R. Wounded

Seeing that the above casualties practically render two Sections out of action it seems to be essential that the personnel of a Machine Gun Company should be increased.

vol. 8

ORIGINAL

WAR DIARY

110 Machine Gun Coy
from Oct 1st – 31st
1916.

Volume 8

Army Form C. 2118.

WAR DIARY
INTELLIGENCE SUMMARY.
(Erase heading not required.)

Instructions regarding War Diaries and Intelligence Summaries are contained in F. S. Regs., Part II. and the Staff Manual respectively. Title pages will be prepared in manuscript.

Place	Date	Hour	Summary of Events and Information	Remarks and references to Appendices
GUEUDECOURT	Oct. 1916 1		Company relieved by 37 Machine Gun Coy and marched back to MONTAUBAN	mg
MONTAUBAN	2		Marched to DERNANCOURT	mg
DERNANCOURT	3		At DERNANCOURT	mg
—	4		Entrained at DERNANCOURT and arrived at LONGPRÉ at 1.32.a.m on the 5th	mg
LONGPRÉ	5	3am	Marched with Brigade to LONGUET	mg
LONGUET	6		In training	mg
—	7	4am	Left LONGUET and marched to PONT REMY where the Coy entrained	mg
BETHUNE	8	6pm.	for BETHUNE which was reached at 3am, 8th Oct 1916	mg
FOUQUEREUIL			The Coy then proceeded to FOUQUEREUIL arriving there at 6/10 a.m.	mg
	9		In billeting	mg
	10		Nos 1 and 2 Sections left for the trenches	mg
VERMELLES	11		Remainder of Coy left FOUQUEREUIL and marched to VERMELLES	mg
	12		Coy relieved 7th Div 25th Machine Gun Coy	mg
	13		Coy in the trenches in the HOHENZOLLERN SECTOR	mg
	14		Do	mg
	15		Do	mg
			Do — An inspection relief took place on this date	mg

WAR DIARY

INTELLIGENCE SUMMARY.

Army Form C. 2118.

Place	Date	Hour	Summary of Events and Information	Remarks and references to Appendices
VERMELLES	16		Company in the trenches in the HOHENZOLLERN SECTOR.	
	17		Do. Situation quiet	
	18		Do. Do.	
	19		Do. Do.	
	20		Do. Do.	
	21		Do. Do.	
	22 }		An inter-section relief took place on this date.	
	23 }		Coy. in trenches in HOHENZOLLERN SECTOR, situation	
	24		normal	
	25			
	26		Do. an inter-section relief took place on this date.	
	27 }		Coy. in the HOHENZOLLERN SECTOR. Situation normal	
	28 }		Do. Do.	
	29		Do. Do.	
	30			
	31			

Vol 9

ORIGINAL

WAR DIARY
- OF -
110 MACHINE GUN COMPANY

FROM 1ST NOVEMBER 1916
TO. 30TH NOVEMBER 1916

Vol. 9.

Army Form C. 2118.

WAR DIARY
or
INTELLIGENCE SUMMARY.
(Erase heading not required.)

Instructions regarding War Diaries and Intelligence Summaries are contained in F. S. Regs., Part II. and the Staff Manual respectively. Title pages will be prepared in manuscript.

Place	Date	Hour	Summary of Events and Information	Remarks and references to Appendices
VERMELLES	Nov 1916 1		Company in the trenches in the HOHENZOLLERN SECTOR Situation normal	W.
"	2		do	W.
"	3		An intersection relief took place on this date	W.
"	4			W.
"	6		Company in the trenches in the HOHENZOLLERN SECTOR Situation normal	W.
"	9			
"	10		Do	
"	11		An intersection relief took place on this date	W.
"	6			
"	15		Company in the trenches in the HOHENZOLLERN SECTOR Situation normal	W.
"	16		Do	W.
"	19 21 22		An intersection relief took place on this date	W.
"			Company in the trenches in the HOHENZOLLERN SECTOR Situation normal	W.
"	23		Do	W.
"	24		An intersection relief took place on this date	W.
"	25		Company in the trenches in the HOHENZOLLERN SECTOR Situation normal	W.
"			do	W.

Army Form C. 2118.

WAR DIARY
or
INTELLIGENCE SUMMARY.
(Erase heading not required.)

Instructions regarding War Diaries and Intelligence
Summaries are contained in F. S. Regs., Part II.
and the Staff Manual respectively. Title pages
will be prepared in manuscript.

Place	Date	Hour	Summary of Events and Information	Remarks and references to Appendices
	1916 Nov.		2	
VERMELLES	26		Company in the trenches on the HOHENZOLLERN SECTOR	
"	27		Company in the trenches on the HOHENZOLLERN SECTOR Situation normal.	
"	28		Do Do	
"	29		Do An intercompany relief took place on this date.	
"	30		Company in the trenches on the HOHENZOLLERN SECTOR Situation normal	

Vol 10

ORIGINAL

WAR DIARY

– OF –

110 MACHINE GUN COMPANY.

FROM 1ST DECEMBER 1916

TO 31ST DECEMBER 1916

VOL. H.

Army Form C. 2118.

110 H M G C 1

WAR DIARY
or
INTELLIGENCE SUMMARY.
(Erase heading not required.)

Instructions regarding War Diaries and Intelligence Summaries are contained in F. S. Regs., Part II. and the Staff Manual respectively. Title pages will be prepared in manuscript.

Place	Date	Hour	Summary of Events and Information	Remarks and references to Appendices
VERMELLES	Dec 1915 1 to 13		Company holding the HOHENZOLLERN SECTOR. 1st Platoon of any importance happened during this period. A general condition of training - this was carried out - and by day the Company in Support Line, Reserve and Headquarters.	
VERMELLES	14		Company relieved by the 61st Machine Gun Company & moved into rest billets in BÉTHUNE. Operation order for this move attached as appendix "A".	
BETHUNE	15 to 19		Company in rest billets. Training carried on.	
BETHUNE	20	10.35 am	Company moved into rest billets in AUCHEL. Operation order for this move attached as appendix "B".	
AUCHEL	21 to 31		Company carried out Routine training. Reis/personal and during this period.	

Appendix "A"

S E C R E T   Copy No. 8

OPERATION ORDERS No. 1B
by
Major A.H.Bowden,   Commanding
110 Machine Gun Company.
———————

1.   The 110th MACHINE GUN COMPANY will be relieved by the 64th MACHINE GUN COMPANY on the morning of the 14th December 1916, and will take over the billets now occupied by No. 64 Machine Gun Company in BETHUNE.

2.   Lieut J. WHITEHEAD with two Signallers will arrange to be at 64 M.G.Company H.Q. BETHUNE at 7 a.m. to take over billets.   He will arrange to meet Sections with guides and shew them their respective billets.   Transport Officer will please arrange for a horse.

3.   Relief will commence at 10.30 a.m. and O.C. No. 2 Section will arrange carrying parties for sections of 64 M.G.Company going in the line, and they will assist sections of 110 M.G. Company coming down.

4.   Guides from each gun emplacement will be at Company Headquarters at 10 a.m.   each guide to clearly understand the number and the route of the gun he is guide for.

5.   The relief will be carried out in the following order and by the following routes :-

　　　　1.   VILLAGE LINE

　　　　　　V. 41   By Road direct.
　　　　　　V.39 & V.40   BARTS ALLEY
　　　　　　RESERVE GUN   HULLUCH ALLEY

　　　　11. RESERVE LINE LEFT.

　　　　　　R.57 & R.58   BARTS ALLEY
　　　　　　R.59 & R.60   QUARRY ALLEY

　　　　111. RESERVE LINE RIGHT.

　　　　　　V.38, R.54   )
　　　　　　R.55 & R.56   )   HULLUCH ALLEY.

6.   On completion of relief each Section will move to Company H.Q., pack their limbers and move off to billets independantly.

7.   Transport Officer will arrange for Limbers to arrive at Company Headquarters as under :-

　　　　No. 2 Section   9   a.m.
　　　　3 Limbers for Q.M.Stores   9.30 a.m.
　　　　H.Q. Limber   )
　　　　Mess Cart   )   11.30 a.m.
　　　　No. 1 Section   )

　　　　No. 4 Section   )
　　　　No. 3 Section   )   1 p.m.

Officers Chargers will arrive with respective limbers.

The C.O's and Adjutant's horses with No. 3 Sections limbers.

8. All maps, trench stores (including gum boots) will be handed over to relieving sections. Lists will be made out in detail, one copy to reach this Office by 9 a.m. 16.12.16.

9. Section Officers will report relief complete on arrival at Company Headquarters.

10. Officers kits will be carried on their Section Limbers and they must arrange to have them ready at the times named in para. 7.

11. Section Officers will ensure that all emplacements (both alternative and battle) are thoroughly in order, and that all dugouts are in a clean condition.
O.C. No. 2 Section will be personally responsible that all billets at H.Q. and ground in vicinity are left clean, also that latrines are covered over and cleaned.

12. The Transport will move to BETHUNE on the 14th instant and will take over the lines now occupied by the transport of 64 Machine Gun Company.

13. Acknowledge.

Parrott
Lt. & Adjt.
110 Machine Gun Company.

Issued at

Copy No. 1 to O.C. No. 1 Section
   2   2
   3   3
   4   4
   5 to O.C. 64 M.G.Company
   6 to Transport Officer.
   7 Office Copy.
   8 War Diary
   9 War Diary

APPENDIX "B"

SECRET   Copy No. 8

OPERATION ORDERS No. 2 B
by
MAJOR A. H. BOWDEN, Commanding
110 Machine Gun Company.

Reference. Map Sheet HAZEBROUCK 5 A. Scale 1/100,000

1. The 110th Machine Gun Company will move into the Reserve Division Area tomorrow the 20th inst. and will take over billets at AUCHEL.

2. The Company will parade in full marching order ready to move off at 10. 35 a.m. (packs will be carried) in the road facing the Company Billet. No. 4 Section on the right.

3. Blankets, Leather Jerkins will be rolled in bundles of ten, clearly labelled, and will be handed in to the Q.M.Stores at 8. 45 a.m.   A motor lorry for the conveyance of above will report at 9 a.m.
All rations in bulk, Q.M. Stores, Transport Stores etc, will also proceed by this lorry. The party detailed to travel by lorry will be as under :- Q.M.S. Cooks and Storeman.
The Q.M.S. will arrange to have dinners ready for 2.30 p.m.

4. The route will be CHOCQUES - PONT DU REVEILLON - ALLOUNGNE - LOZINGHEM - AUCHEL.

5. The H.Q. Limber will report to the Orderly Room at 10.15 a.m. and will when packed proceed to the Officers Mess to pick up the C.O's kit.
The Mess Cart will report to the O.M.Corporal at 9.45 a.m.
The above two vehicles will fall in at the end of the column when the Company pass.

6. Transport will march in the rear of the Company and will be ready to move off at 10. 35 a.m.   The head of the transport being opposite the present orderly room at this hour.   Officers horses will parade at the same hour.

7. Breakfasts tomorrow will be at 9 a.m. and billets etc will be thoroughly clean by 9.45 a.m. when the C.O. will inspect them. Section Officers will be responsible for the cleanliness of their Section billets.

8. The Guard will be dismounted at 7 a.m.

9. Steel helmets will be worn and caps will be carried in the pack out of sight.

Parrott
Lt. & Adjt.
110 Machine Gun Company.

Copy No.1 to O.C. No. 1 Sect.   Copy No.2 to O.C. No. 2 Sectn.
         3   3   4   4
         5 Transport Officer
         6 C.S.M.
         7 Office Copy.
         8 War Diary
         9 War Diary

Vol XI

ORIGINAL

WAR DIARY
- OF -
110 MACHINE GUN COMPANY

From 1st JANUARY 1917
To 31st JANUARY 1917

VOL #2

SHEET. I

WAR DIARY
or
INTELLIGENCE SUMMARY.
(Erase heading not required.)

110th Machine Gun Army Form C. 2118.

Instructions regarding War Diaries and Intelligence Summaries are contained in F. S. Regs., Part II. and the Staff Manual respectively. Title pages will be prepared in manuscript.

Place	Date	Hour	Summary of Events and Information	Remarks and references to Appendices
AUCHEL	JAN 1 1917 25.		Company in Training. Nothing of note for this period.	
AUCHEL	26.		Company receives warning orders for relief of M.G. Coy in L.O.O.S Sector on the 29-1-17. The O.C. Company visits the Sector to be taken over on this date.	
AUCHEL	26.	9 p.m.	Orders received to suspend any further action as regards the relief.	
AUCHEL	27	3.45 a.m.	Orders received for Company to stand by ready for an immediate move.	
AUCHEL	27	4.30 a.m.	Orders received for part of Reinforcement to proceed at 9 a.m. & warning the Company are a immediate move. Train to be notified later.	
AUCHEL	27	2.30 p.m.	Operation orders for the move by rail received.	
AUCHEL	28	12.30 a.m.	Company entrained at HAZEBROUCK Station 16 officers at H.Q. of HAZEBROUCK, ammunition & transport at 9.30 a.m. The HAZEBROUCK order being ammunition	

SHEET. II

Army Form C. 2118.

WAR DIARY
or
INTELLIGENCE SUMMARY.
(Erase heading not required.)

Instructions regarding War Diaries and Intelligence Summaries are contained in F. S. Regs., Part II. and the Staff Manual respectively. Title pages will be prepared in manuscript.

Place	Date	Hour	Summary of Events and Information	Remarks and references to Appendices
	JAN 19/17 18			
PROVEN	18	Noon	and orders to bivouac at PROVEN substituted.	8.
			Debivouacd at PROVEN and marched to billets in BRIEL. The route being PROVEN – WATOU – DROGLANDT – WINNEZEELE – BRIEL. arrived about 4 p.m.	8.
BRIEL	29 31		Company training. No events for our invisible move.	8.

WAR DIARY
or
INTELLIGENCE SUMMARY.
(Erase heading not required.)

Army Form C. 2118.

110th Company M.G. Corps
110th Machine Gun Company

Vol 12

Place	Date	Hour	Summary of Events and Information	Remarks and references to Appendices
BRIEL	FEB 1917. 1. to 12		Company in billets at BRIEL. Nothing to report in this sector. BELGIAN line. HQ YPRES, YPRES etc reconnoitred by the C.O. during this period.	
- " -	13	6.15am	C/E BRIEL and marched to PROVEN Station where the Company entrained for CHOCQUES. Train arrived at 11.44 pm and Company C/E CHOCQUES 4 pm.	
		4 pm	Detrained and marched to BETHUNE where Company was billeted for the night.	
BETHUNE	14	8am	Company left BETHUNE to relieve the 18th Machine Gun Coy in the HOHENZOLLERN Sector, relief completed by 8pm. Coy HQ established at VERMELLES BREWERY. Company in HOHENZOLLERN SECTOR. Nothing of importance to report. Resumed during this period.	
VERMELLES	15 to 28			

APPENDIX "A"

<u>SECRET</u>　　　　　　　　　　　　　　　　　　　　Copy No. 7

Reference Operation Orders No. B.4 issued to-day, the following alterations will be made.

      Para 3.   The train will leave PROVEN 12.34 arriving at CHOCQUES 15.52

      Para. 8   The time for parade will now be 6.15 a.m. The Transport will pass the starting point at this time.

(signed) Parrott
Lt. & Adjt.
110 Machine Gun Company.

S E C R E T   　　　　　　　　　　　　　　　　　Copy No. 7

OPERATION ORDERS No. B.4
by
Major A. H. BOWDEN,   Commanding
110 Machine Gun Company.

Reference Map 1/100,000 HAZEBROUCK.

1.　　The 21st Division has been ordered to return to the 1 Corps Area.

2.　　The 110 Machine Gun Company will take over the HOHENZOLLERN SECTOR on the 15th February 1917.
　　　　No. 4 Section will take over the RIGHT SECTOR
　　　　No. 1 Section will take over the LEFT SECTOR
　　　　No. 2 Section will take over the VILLAGE LINE
　　　　No. 3 Section will be in RESERVE at Company H.Q.

3.　　The Company and Transport (less Transport enumerated in para. 4) will proceed by train on the 13th February 1917 leaving PROVEN at 4.0 p.m. arriving CHOCQUES at 18.2.

4.　　The following Transport will proceed by road on the 13th inst.
　　　　Train Transport.
　　　　Two G.S.Limbered Wagons.
The starting point for the road party will be the CROSS ROADS SOUTH OF THE "W" IN WINNEZEELE, and time of passing 10.30 a.m. The 110th Infantry Brigade Transport moving by road will march under Capt. DIXON, 7th Battn Leicestershire Regiment.

5.　　One blanket per man will be taken on the train with the men. The remainder will be carried in bulk.

6.　　One Motor Lorry for Blankets and Q.M.Stores will be at WINNEZEELE CHURCH at 3.30 a.m. on the morning of the 13th instant. O.C. No. 1 Section will detail a guide to be at this point at 3.30 a.m. to guide the Lorry to Company Headquarters.

7.　　All blankets rolled in bundles of ten and clearly marked will be stacked outside the billets by 3.30 a.m. All Quartermaster Stores will be ready for loading at the same hour. Any Transport stores which require conveying by this Lorry will be stacked at the entrance to the Transport Lines at 3.30 a.m. when the Lorry will pick them up.

8.　　The Company will parade ready to move off at 10.15 a.m. on the 13th instant. Packs will be carried. Leather Jerkins will be rolled in bundles of ten and carried on Section Limbers. The head of the Transport Column will pass the starting point (Company H.Q.J.10.a.80.50. Ref. Sheet 27 N.E.1/20,000)

9.　　The Orderly Officer for the day will inspect all billets and latrines before the Company moves, and will report that they are correct.

10.　ACKNOWLEDGE

　　　　　　　　　　　　　　　　　　　　　Lt. & Adjt.
　　　　　　　　　　　　　　　　　　　110 Machine Gun Company.

Copy No. 1 to O.C. 1 Section　　　　Copy No. 2 to O.C. 2 Section.
　　　　3   3　　　　　　　　　　　　　　　4   4
　　　　5 Transport Officer　　　　　　　　6 Office copy
　　　　7 War Diary　　　　　　　　　　　　8 War Diary

Vol 13

- ORIGINAL -

War
- of -
Diary

110 Machine Gun Company

From 1st March 1917
To 31st March 1917

Vol. 14

ORIGINAL

Army Form C. 2118.

WAR DIARY
or
INTELLIGENCE SUMMARY.
(Erase heading not required.)

110th M.G. Coy

Instructions regarding War Diaries and Intelligence Summaries are contained in F. S. Regs., Part II. and the Staff Manual respectively. Title pages will be prepared in manuscript.

Place	Date	Hour	Summary of Events and Information	Remarks and references to Appendices
VERNELLES	1924 MARCH 1st		Company in HOHENZOLLERN SECTOR	188
"	" 2nd		Company relieved by 2nd Machine Gun Squadron, Sections as relieved marching to billets in NOYELLES.	188
NOYELLES	" 3rd to 15th		Company in billets at NOYELLES. Working party supplied each day.	188
"	" 16th		Company left NOYELLES to relieve the 2nd Machine Gun Squadron in the HOHENZOLLERN SECTOR. Operation Order No B 6 attached. All Sections in the line.	188
VERNELLES	" 17th to 25th		Company in HOHENZOLLERN SECTOR	188
"	" 26th		Company relieved by 91st and 204th Machine Gun Companies, Sections as relieved marching to billets in NOYELLES.	188
NOYELLES	" 27th 28th		Company in billets at NOYELLES.	188
"	" 29th		Company paraded at 7.30 a.m. and proceeded by Motor Buses to LARBRET. Marched from LARBRET to HUMBERCAMP, and billeted in huts.	188
HUMBERCAMP	" 30th to 31st		Company training at HUMBERCAMP.	188

SECRET Copy No. 4/10

OPERATION ORDERS No. B.6
by
Major A. H. BOWDEN,   Commanding
110 Machine Gun Company.

---

1. The 110th Machine Gun Company less one Section now occupying the VILLAGE LINE, and two guns at R.53 and V.37 already attached to the 2nd Brigade Machine Gun Squadron, will relieve the 2nd Brigade Machine Gun Squadron tomorrow March 16th 1917.

2. The relief will be carried out as follows :-
   No. 1 Section enumerated above will arrange to occupy the following gun positions on being relieved :-
   RESERVE GUN will relieve R. 56
   V. 38   "   "   CENTRAL KEEP
   V. 40   "   "   V. 40
   V. 39   "   "   V. 39
Section Headquarters will remain at V. 39.
   No 2 Section will constitute the LEFT SECTOR and will relieve the following guns :-
       R. 57
       R. 58
       R. 59
       R. 60
until further orders.
R. 56 will also be under Section Officer of LEFT SECTOR for administration and discipline. Section Headquarters will be situated in the original Section Officer's Headquarters in dugout in BARTS ALLEY.
   No. 3 Section will constitute the RIGHT SECTOR and will relieve as under :-
       R. 55
       R. 54
       R. 53   (already relieved)
       FARMERS LANE
   Section Headquarters will be at :-
   No. 4 Section will constitute VILLAGE LINE RIGHT and will relieve as follows :-
       RESERVE GUN
       V. 38
       V. 37   (already relieved)
       V. 35
   Section Headquarters will be at :-

3. The relief will commence at 10.45 a.m. from THE BREWERY VERMELLES, where guides for all gun teams will report at that hour.

4. On relief the following stores will be taken over :-
       10 belt boxes per gun.
       Gun boots.
       List of Targets
       All Maps
       Order Boards
       Range Cards.

5. The list of trench stores taken over by Section Officers will be sent to Company Headquarters not later than 12 noon 17th instant.

6. Unexpired portion of rations for the 16th instant will be carried on the men.

7. Section Officers will report relief complete in writing immediately they have taken over.

8. The Transport Officer will arrange transport as follows :-

    No. 3 Section.   2 Limbers at 7.45 a.m.
    No. 4 "   2 " at 8 a.m.
    No. 2 "   2 " at 8.15 a.m.
    No. 1 "   1 Limber containing No. 1 Section's spare equipment at 8.15 a.m. O.C. No. 2 Section will be responsible for the unloading of No. 1 Section's spare equipment.
    Two Limber for Q.M.Stores at 8.45 a.m.
    Mess Cart and Headquarter Limber to report at Officers Mess at 10 a.m.

9. The Transport Officer will arrange to send Company rations for the 17th instant to THE BREWERY early on the afternoon of the 16th instant, and those of the 2nd Machine Gun Squadron to our original Company Quartermaster Stores at NOYELLES some time after 3 p.m. on the 16th instant.

10. The Company will move off by Sections a quarter of an hour after the time stated above for limbers to arrive. On arrival at THE BREWERY they will unload all their equipment and proceed to bathe at the baths VERMELLES.

11. The route into VERMELLES will be via PHILOSOPHE, unless the weather is sufficiently misty to enable the short cut to be used.

12. The Orderly Officer will be responsible that the Company billets, latrines etc. are left in a clean condition and in good order.

13. ACKNOWLEDGE.

                                              2/Lt. & Adjt.
                                          110 Machine Gun Company.

Issued at   p.m. 15th March 1917.

    Copy No. 1 - Headquarters, 110th Infantry Brigade.
           2 - O.C. 2nd Machine Gun Squadron.
           3 - O.C. No. 1 Section.
           4 - O.C. No. 2 Section.
           5 - O.C. No. 3 Section.
           6 - O.C. No. 4 Section.
           7 - Transport Officer.
           8 - Office Copy
           9 - War Diary
          10 - War Diary.

SHEET I.

Army Form C. 2118.

WAR DIARY
or
INTELLIGENCE SUMMARY.

110th Coy M.G. Corps

(Erase heading not required.)

Place	Date	Hour	Summary of Events and Information	Remarks and references to Appendices
HUMBERCAMP	April 1		Company Resting at HUMBERCAMP.	
-"-	"2		Company Resting at HUMBERCAMP. Lt W.F. PARROTT joined the Company from 62nd Machine Gun Company.	
HAMELINCOURT	"3		Nos 2 and 4 Sections marched to BOISLEUX-AU-MONT via POMMIER, BIENVILLERS-AU-BOIS, MONCHY-AU-BOIS, ADINFER, BOIRY ST MARTIN. Sections arrived at BOISLEUX-AU-MONT at 2 p.m. and took over from 64th Machine Gun Company. Gun positions were supplies in the village of BOISLEUX-AU-MONT and east of the ARRAS-ALBERT Railway, the line then held being BOISLEUX-AU-MONT — HAMELINCOURT. Nos 1 and 3 Sections marched to HAMELINCOURT via POMMIER, BIENVILLERS-AU-BOIS, MONCHY-AU-BOIS, ADINFER. Arrived at HAMELINCOURT at 6 p.m. where Company Headquarters were established, and Sections bivouacked.	
-"-	"4		No 1 Section attached to the 1st Batt LEICESTER REGT. and succeeded in the line. No 3 Section attached to the 6th Batt LEICESTER REGT. and proceeded to the line taking up position N.W. of CROISILLES on the sunken road.	
-"-	"5		Two guns of No 1 Section took up positions in the northern outskirts of CROISILLES, the remaining two guns being placed South of the village.	

WAR DIARY or INTELLIGENCE SUMMARY

Army Form C. 2118.

SHEET II

Place	Date	Hour	Summary of Events and Information	Remarks and references to Appendices
HAMELINCOURT	April 16		The guard of No 4 Section withdrawn to Company Headquarters at HAMELINCOURT, No 2 Section being left in position to defend the village.	
	"	7 am	2nd Lieut F. Abney joined the Company.	
	"	8 am	No 4 Section and A and C Companies of the 8th LEICESTER REGT. placed under the command of CAPT. J. BURDETT and ordered to but 8th Infantry Brigade. They proceeded to the line and took up position in sunken road N.W. of CROISILLES.	
			No 1 Section ordered no casualty in this duel — No 405608 PTE BAKER. R.T. wounded.	
			8th Infantry Brigade attacked and ordered on exploring flanks of the HINDENBURG LINE. About 5.30 pm A and C Companies 8th LEICESTER REGT and No 4 Section took up position from the sunken road N.W. of CROISILLES to the HINDENBURG LINE, where they lay in and formed a defensive flank to the right of the attack. No 4 Section sustained one casualty, No 3310 PTE. ALLEN. B. killed.	
	"	10 pm	In the evening at 6.30 pm the enemy retook from front line our advance moved forward to a position along the valley T9 & 15 T9 6 (Sheet 51B SW). The enemy did not attempt to counter-attack and cleared and at about 7 pm many of our troops withdrew.	

SHEET III

WAR DIARY
or
INTELLIGENCE SUMMARY.
(Erase heading not required.)

Army Form C. 2118.

Place	Date	Hour	Summary of Events and Information	Remarks and references to Appendices
	9.4.18.		+ took up a position on a ridge running Eastwards & running approx. from T.S.c. 30.20. to T.4.b.30.50. Men of the 9th Durham Regt came up from Flesquières about T.S.c. 30.80. frontage is about 1500 yds and we were - having a position at junction of Flesquières and advanced posts on depth 10 yards. The situation at this time was that Plus - the enemy had neglected these Pois (Gurd Line (HINDENBURG LINE) on the night - 8/9 and the flanking trenches which the enemy have observation and which hinders our own left, & the left flank of his advance left unprotected. Towards evening communication was established with Phe left comm. established about T.2.d, b left ufront the 11½ M.Fan. who were holding a trench system extending on way, on Cavalry in No 1 Section. N° 46747 Pte T. G. MIDDLETON came -	
			During the morning the enemy were driven to leave a considerable line but in any other Particular were inactive.	

WAR DIARY or INTELLIGENCE SUMMARY

Army Form C. 2118.

SHEET XI

Place	Date	Hour	Summary of Events and Information	Remarks and references to Appendices
	2/9/17		At this point Sniper were very active, the same snipers accounting for many quite a lot of our casualties. HQ & our attack up to this line were well advanced with the bulk of the men of two Sections in their [?] support line were well [?] position [?] ahead advanced from rear [?] [?] [?]	
	Ap 15	3 pm	Owing to [?] [?] by [?] and the Plt on [?] two guns of [?] a casualty of Pt. 6 of Pltn Rank team were [?] advance. The advance by [?] [?] [?] our front of the [?] [?] They decided is held [?] at [?] of the [?] [?] [?] [?] [?] [?] [?] Stokes of Lewis Gunners in Plt [?] [?] [?] [?] [?] [?] Pl & [?] which the enemy [?] [?] [?] to advance is also [?] under [?] [?] [?] Pt. HINDENBURG LINE. Two Casualties were evident 2/Lt MURRAY and 10 Pigeon N° 82762 Pte T. IRONS being wounded that N° 21762 Pte T. IRONS killed.	

SHEET V

WAR DIARY or INTELLIGENCE SUMMARY

Army Form C. 2118.

Place	Date	Hour	Summary of Events and Information	Remarks and references to Appendices
	4/6/13		On this date Coy. HQ & No 1 Section moved forward to ST LEGER, but were unable to move heads to HAMELINCOURT. The same morning, owing to the attacks on the HINDENBURG line having failed, No 1 Section was relieved by No 2 Section.	
CROISELLES	5/6/17		No 1 Section came out of the line intending to carry HQ at 3am. No 2 & 3 Sections were relieved by two sections of the 100th Tunnelling Coy. Coy Compound of the Section then the 100 T.C. Coy Tunnellers took to BAILLEULVAL where remained during this	
	6/6/16	10 am	Compound in training during this period	
	22nd		2/Lt. F.C. KIDD joined on the 20/5/17 and 11 other ranks	
	4/6/22		Compound marched to BOIRY ST MARTIN and bivouacked.	
	14/6/24		Compound remained at BOIRY ST MARTIN.	
	4/6/25		Compound marched from BOIRY ST MARTIN & bivouacked N.W. of ST LEGER. Nos 2 & 3 Sections relieved two sections of the	

SHEET VI

Army Form C. 2118.

WAR DIARY
or
INTELLIGENCE SUMMARY.
(Erase heading not required.)

Place	Date	Hour	Summary of Events and Information	Remarks and references to Appendices
	4/25		100th Machine Gun Coy in CROISILLES sector on the right.	
	4/26/16		Situation remained unaltered. Refixing of emplacements.	
	4/27		No 53381 Pte Goulding F.W. admitted.	
	4/28		Nos 3 & 5 Stations relieved by two Sections of the 171st Machine Gun Coy.	
			Considerable work in completion of new emplacements under Regt Quartermaster Sgt BOYELLES. Company in Reserve at BOYELLES.	
			APPENDICES	
	4/30		These militia vehicles were employed for operations on the 9th & 15th. The accounts of these events are furnished by Pim... are attached as appendix "A".	

ORIGINAL

Vol 15

(5)

WAR DIARY
- OF -

110 MACHINE GUN COMPANY.

From 1st May 1917
To 31st May 1917

Vol. 16

Sheet 1

Army Form C. 2118.

WAR DIARY
or
INTELLIGENCE SUMMARY.
(Erase heading not required.)

Nott: Mil [?]

Place	Date	Hour	Summary of Events and Information	Remarks and references to Appendices
BOYELLES	1917 May 1st		Company in tunnels at BOYELLES. No 4 Section proceeded to the line and took up position in the HINDENBURG SUPPORT TRENCH. The Section sustained three casualties on this night. No 5394 Sgt Walker, No 9993 Sgt HARRISON and No 5123 L/Cpl BUTLER — all being wounded. Two casualties also occurred in the transport section, three bombs of which had been sent to the R.E. Dump at T.4.b.40.50. (Ref. Sheet 51B S.W. 4th.) The Dump was shelled and No 5794 Pte DUFFY was killed, and No L/Cpl BLACKHURST wounded.	
HINDENBURG LINE	May 2nd		Nos 1, 2, and 3 Sections proceeded to the line, and Advanced Company Headquarters were established in the HINDENBURG SUPPORT TRENCH at T.5.L.95.15, two gun teams of No 2 Section being held here in reserve. Nos 1 and 3 Sections were attached to the 9th and 9th Batt Leicestershire Regt respectively, and positions were taken up in the BROWN LINE running on a N to S work socally direction from T.a 60.60 to T.a 15.40.	
—	May 3rd 3.25 a.m.		The 110th Infantry Brigade attacked FONTAINE-LEZ-CROISILLES, but the enemy put up a spirited resistance, and progress was very slow. Machine Guns were unable to make any noticeable advance. The some of the guns went around and out out to bring offensive fire to bear on the edge of FONTAINE WOOD.	

WAR DIARY
or
INTELLIGENCE SUMMARY.

Army Form C. 2118.

Place	Date	Hour	Summary of Events and Information	Remarks and references to Appendices
HINDENBURG LINE	1917 May 3	11.15 a.m.	110th Infantry Brigade consolidated position won, until such time as the attack could be resumed.	
		6 p.m.	Two guns of No 1 Section pushed forward to position approximately T6b 30.75 and T6b 55.90.	
		7.15 a.m.	Attack renewed, but was not successful	
		10.55 p.m.	110th Infantry Brigade withdrew their Battalions from the advanced position, the withdrawal being covered by our Machine Guns. The Brigade occupied the BROWN LINE and positions in rear of it. Eight of the Company's Machine Guns were now in the BROWN LINE, the remaining eight being situated as follows:— Two guns of No 1 Section T6b 30.75 and T6b 55.90. Two guns of No 2 Section at Advanced Company HQ T5d 95.75 (both in reserve) Four guns of No 4 Section at T6d 70.75, T6d 60.55, N36c 35.40 and N36c 70.90 All guns were held in readiness to meet an expected counter attack, which however did not materialise, and the remainder of the night was comparatively quiet. Casualties sustained during the day:— Killed. No 58019 Pte. HUTCHINSON. No 6022 Pte. KITCHEN. No 22234 Pte. MOUSLEY.	

Army Form C. 2118.

Sheet 3

Instructions regarding War Diaries and Intelligence Summaries are contained in F.S. Regs., Part II. and the Staff Manual respectively. Title pages will be prepared in manuscript.

WAR DIARY
INTELLIGENCE SUMMARY.
(Erase heading not required.)

Place	Date	Hour	Summary of Events and Information	Remarks and references to Appendices
HINDENBURG LINE	April 3rd (contd.)		WOUNDED – N° 5584 Sgt SONGER, N° 5584 Sgt POULTER, N° 5887 Cpl. TRAINER. D° 9956 Pte CUNDALL, N° 45444 Pte MANNEN.	[initials]
—	April 4th		Situation unaltered. Company H.Q., Machine Gun Party and transport moved to Railway Embankment N.W. of ST LEGER, and bivouacked.	[initials]
ST LEGER	April 5th		Company relieved in HINDENBURG LINE by 62nd Machine Gun Company. N°1 and 4 Sections, and two guns of N° 2 Section proceed to Company H.Q. situated at the Railway Embankment N.W. of ST LEGER. N° 3 Section and two guns of N° 2 Section proceeded to take up position N.E. of CROISILLES.	[initials]
—	April 6th		Disposition of the Company unaltered.	[initials]
—	April 7th		do. do.	[initials]
—	April 8th		do. – Section relief. N° 3 & 4 Sections and one gun of N° 2 Section in the line, N° 1 Section relieved a section of the 62nd Machine Gun Company on CROISILLES, the latter moving to Company H.Q. and being attached to this Company.	[initials]
—	April 9th		Disposition of the Company unaltered.	[initials]
BIENVILLERS	April 10th April 11th		Company relieved by 100th Machine Gun Company and marched to rest billets in BIENVILLERS-AU-BOIS.	[initials]

Army Form C. 2118.

WAR DIARY
INTELLIGENCE SUMMARY.
(Erase heading not required.)

Place	Date	Hour	Summary of Events and Information	Remarks and references to Appendices
BIENVILLERS AU BOIS	1919 May 13th		Company training at BIENVILLERS. During this period the H.Q. Company Major A.H. BOWDEN left on four days leave to PARIS. He left on May 19th and returned on May 22nd.	
	May 31st		Gallant work was done by No. 46484 Cpl (now Sgt) J. PENNINGTON No. 9986. No. 5569 Pte H.G. MAYSTON No. 85055 Pte R. DEAN. No. 65903 L/Cpl M. KINSELLA No. 2229 Pte I. EDGE No. 8205 Pte J. NOLAN. Three of the above Sergt PENNINGTON L/Cpl KINSELLA and Pte NOLAN received the Military Medal for their good work during the trenches on May 3rd and the remainder received the Divisional Commanders Complimentary Card.	

Army Form W. 3121.

Schedule No. (To be left blank)	Unit	Brigade.	Division.	Corps.	Date of Recommendation.
	110th Machine Gun Company	21st	VII		

Regtl. No.	Rank and Name	Action for which commended	Recommended by	Honour or Reward	(To be left blank)
9993	Lance Sergt WILLIAM HARRISON	During the recent operations Sergt HARRISON was in charge of one of the gun teams of No. 4 Section. The position of his gun was most important, on account of its nearness to the enemy's front line, and the danger of counter attacks. After the advance on the 9th April Sergt HARRISON opened fire on the enemy's wire where numerous snipers were hidden. By means of occasional bursts of fire Sergt HARRISON kept the snipers in check until the infantry had dug in. Many more casualties would have resulted but for his prompt action. Again on the 11th April when the enemy counter attacked on our left, our infantry withdrew from a portion of the trench where Sergt HARRISON's gun was; he promptly removed his gun a short distance to a better position where he could enfilade the enemy as they advanced, and brought fire to bear on them, thus saving a critical situation. Also on the second advance of the 13th April Sergt HARRISON went forward with the first wave of infantry. He advanced with his team through a heavy barrage, and, although one man of the team was killed, he arrived at the objective before many of the infantry who were held up in the open by snipers and machine gun fire. Sergt HARRISON gallantly brought his team into action and maintained valuable covering fire on enemy positions until our infantry were established in the new position. I very strongly recommend Sergt HARRISON for devotion to duty and gallant conduct.			

APPENDIX X.

Army Form W. 3121.

Schedule No. (To be left blank)	Unit	Regtl. No.	Rank and Name	Action for which commended	Recommended by	Honour or Reward	(To be left blank)
	110 Machine Gun Company	9036	Private ELIAS CUNDALL	I recommend Pte CUNDALL for great coolness in action, and devotion to duty on the 9th and 14th April. On the 9th April when it was most essential for his gun to continue firing, he volunteered to fetch belt boxes from a place several hundred yards away; he did this in spite of the snipers who were very active and deadly at this time. On the 11th April, during an attack by the enemy, he gallantly stuck to his post, being No. 2 on the gun team, and bravely did his duty, thus materially assisting to keep his gun firing at a critical time. Immediately afterwards he volunteered to take a message to his Section Officer, and to bring up more ammunition. Pte CUNDALL in order to deliver this message, had to pass through a very heavy artillery barrage caused by our own guns, which were at this time falling short. Pte CUNDALL by his coolness and personal courage was able to give the utmost assistance to his team Commander, Sergt HARRISON and to Pte LEWIS who was No. 1 on his team.			

110TH Brigade.   21st Division.   VII Corps.

Army Form W. 3121.

Schedule No.	Unit	Regtl. No.	Rank and Name	Action for which commended	Recommended by	Honour or Reward	(To be left blank)
	110 Machine Gun Company	25161	Private WALTER LEWIS	I strongly recommend Pte LEWIS for gallant conduct in the field on April 9th. He was No. 1 in his team. As soon as the team had arrived at its new position after the advance, he immediately got his gun into action, though being fired at continually by snipers at close range, and being exposed to machine gun fire. He gallantly kept his gun firing during the time the infantry were consolidating the position, and kept the enemy's fire in check. Also on the 11th April when the enemy attacked on our left, and our infantry had to withdraw, he brought his gun out of action and took up a new position under Sergt HARRISON's orders, and brought fire to bear on the enemy. Later he brought up (guided) a party of our bombers through our own artillery barrage which was falling short. Pte LEWIS was instrumental at this time in turning a critical incident to our advantage. His action was most praiseworthy.			

110th Brigade. 21st Division. VII Corps.

ORIGINAL

WAR DIARY 9/6/16
OF
110TH MACHINE GUN COY
FROM JUNE 1ST 1917 TO JUNE 30TH 1917

VOL. IV.

Sheet 1.

Army Form C. 2118.

WAR DIARY
INTELLIGENCE SUMMARY.
(Erase heading not required.)

110th Machine Gun Coy

Instructions regarding War Diaries and Intelligence Summaries are contained in F. S. Regs., Part II. and the Staff Manual respectively. Title pages will be prepared in manuscript.

Place	Date	Hour	Summary of Events and Information	Remarks and references to Appendices
BIENVILLERS-AU-BOIS	1917 June 1st		The Company paraded at 6.45 a.m. and marched by cross-country track to MOYENNEVILLE, where they occupied tents in Camp "E".	
MOYENNEVILLE	June 2nd to June 6th		The Company in Divisional Reserve at Camp "E", MOYENNEVILLE.	
ST. LEGER	June 7th		The Company relieved 62nd Machine Gun Company, and took over the RIGHT SECTOR of the Divisional front, running N.W. from approximately U.13.d.90.10 to U.17.a. central (Ref.ce Sheet 51.B S.W. 1/20,000). Company Headquarters were established at the Railway Embankment N.W. of ST LEGER at T.20.d.8.2. All Sections were read in the line, and were disposed as follows:— Front Line — No 4 Section Intermediate Line — No 2 and 3 Section Reserve Line — No 1 Section.	
"	June 8/9th night		Two Gun teams of No 3 Section withdrawn to Company Headquarters. Dispositions of the Company unaltered, and situation fairly normal. Intimated shelling by the enemy caused a few casualties but none fatal. On the afternoon of the 13th an inter-Section Relief was carried out, after which Sections were	
"	June 9th to June 13th			

Sheet 2.

Army Form C. 2118.

WAR DIARY
of
INTELLIGENCE SUMMARY.
(Erase heading not required.)

Instructions regarding War Diaries and Intelligence Summaries are contained in F. S. Regs., Part II. and the Staff Manual respectively. Title pages will be prepared in manuscript.

Place	Date	Hour	Summary of Events and Information	Remarks and references to Appendices
ST LEGER	1917 June 13th		deployed as follows:-	
			Front Line - No 3 Section	
			Intermediate Line - No 1 and 2 Sections (2 gun teams only of No 2 Section)	
			Reserve Line - No 4 Section	
"	June 14th		Dispositions unaltered	
"	June 15th		Two and a half Sections (Ten guns) of 62nd Machine Gun Company attached to this Company to assist in the attack on TUNNEL TRENCH to take place on the 16th June.	
"	June 16th		The 110th Infantry Brigade attacked TUNNEL TRENCH. The attack was unsuccessful.	
"	June 17th		Two and a half Sections of 62nd Machine Gun Company were withdrawn, and proceeded to their Headquarters.	
"	June 18th		Dispositions of the Company unaltered	
"	June 19th		Company relieved by 19th Machine Gun Company, and proceeded to Camp "E" MOYENNEVILLE.	
MOYENNEVILLE	June 20th		Company relieved at MOYENNEVILLE by the 100th Machine Gun Company, and proceeded to billets in BLAIRVILLE.	
BLAIRVILLE	June 21st to June 30th		Company training at BLAIRVILLE.	

Sheet 3

WAR DIARY

INTELLIGENCE SUMMARY.

Army Form C. 2118.

Place	Date	Hour	Summary of Events and Information	Remarks and references to Appendices
	1917			
BAHIREVILLE	June 30th		The Company sustained the casualties during its tour of duty in the line, six other ranks being wounded.	
			APPENDICES.	
			No 1. Operation Order for relief of 62nd Machine Gun Company by 10th Machine Gun Company on June 1st.	
			No 2. Operation Order for Inter-Section Relief on 13th inst.	
			No 3. Machine Gun Appendices with reference to the attack on TUNNEL TRENCH on June 16th.	

APPENDIX I.

SECRET								Copy No. 8

OPERATION ORDERS
by
Major A. H. BOWDEN, Commanding
110th Machine Gun Company.

Reference :-   Sheet 51.b.S.W. 1/20,000.

1. The Company will relieve the 62nd Machine Gun Company tomorrow the 7th instant.

2. Sections will be disposed as follows :-
    Front Line			No. 4 Section.
    Intermediate Line		Nos. 2 and 3 Sections.
    Reserve Line			No. 1 Section.

3. Guides will meet Sections as under :-
    No. 1 Section at Railway Embankment (level crossing) T.21.c.05.00 at 8 p.m.
    No. 2 Section at CROISILLES CHURCH at 5 p.m.
    No. 3 Section at Railway Embankment T.21.c.05.00 at 9 p.m.
    No. 4 Section at CROISILLES CHURCH at 4 p.m.

4. Sections will move off independently from present Headquarters in accordance with the above times, accompanied by their two gun limbers.

5. After relief is complete each Section will return four intelligent men to Company Headquarters. These men will be used as runners.

6. It is most important that when reporting relief complete to Company Headquarters, Section Officers state the number of belt boxes handed over to them by the Section relieved.

7. Section Officers must ensure that there is a Range Card in each of their gun positions.

8. On the night of the 8th instant, O.C. No. 2 Section will be responsible for forwarding the rations of No. 4 Section. O.C. No. 4 Section will send his ration party to No. 2 Section who will be in the QUARRIES in front of CROISILLES.

9. Packs will not be taken into the line, they will be stored with the Transport. Greatcoats and waterproof sheets will be carried by the men.

10. The S.O.S. Signal will be a succession of RED Rockets. The Signal to our Artillery to lengthen range will be a succession of WHITE Rockets.

11. Company Headquarters will be established tomorrow at the Railway Embankment T.20.d.8.2.

						Lt. & Adjt.
						110 Machine Gun Company.

Copy No. 1 - O.C. 62 M.G.Coy.		Copy No. 6 to T.O.
       2 - O.C. No. 1 Section			 7 Office Copy
       3 - 2				 8 War Diary
       4 - 3				 9 War Diary.
       5 -   4

APPENDIX 2.

SECRET Copy No. 6

OPERATION ORDERS
by
Major A. H. BOWDEN,   Commanding
110 Machine Gun Company.

---

1. An Intersection Relief will be carried out as follows on the afternoon of the 13th instant :-
    No. 3 Section will relieve No. 4 Section
    " 1   "   "   "   " No. 2   "

Disposition after relief will be as follows :-
    No. 3 Section in the Front Line
    No. 1 Section in the Intermediate Line
    No. 2 Section - two guns in the vicinity of CROISILLES and 2 guns at Company Headquarters.
    No. 4 Section - in Reserve Line west of CROISILLES.

2. The relief will be carried out as follows :-
    No. 4 Section guides will rendezvous at the QUARRIES, outside No. 2 Section Headquarters at 4 p.m. Lieut AINSCOUGH will meet O.C. No. 3 Section at the Church in CROISILLES with his gun teams, guns, spare parts and first aid cases, having previously dumped his two tripods and belt boxes at his Headquarters in charge of Private CARR, who will report to him there on the morning of the 13th instant. O.C. No. 3 Section will then detail Lieut AINSCOUGH to report to Company Headquarters.

    In order to avoid unnecessary exposure, O.C. No. 3 Section will only take up one limber as far as the QUARRIES. No. 4 Section will utilise the same limber after completion of relief. Every effort must be made by both Sections concerned not to keep this Limber waiting at the QUARRIES any longer than can possibly be helped. O.C. No. 2 Section will advise O.C. No. 3 Section the most suitable spot for this limber to remain for the above period.

    In order to ensure a quick and satisfactory relief, O.C. No. 4 Section will remain behind until O.C. No. 3 Section is thoroughly acquainted with the line, and all correspondence and dispositions issued from those Headquarters are thoroughly understood, after which, O.C. No. 4 Section will return personally to Company Headquarters. O.C. No. 4 Section will detail his sub-Section Officer to return with the Section as quickly as possible to the Cross Tracks at T.22.c.45.50. The route will be - CROISILLES - St. LEGER - then past the St. LEGER Cemetery and up the Sunken Road in T.22.c. The Limber will be unloaded, and guides to the positions, which all N.C.O's and No. 1's of the gun teams of No. 4 Section must be thoroughly acquainted with, will await this limber at the above Cross Tracks. The Guide will first conduct 2/Lt. J.C.KIDD and his gun teams to their bivouacs in Sunken Road at T.22.d.20.85. All Section equipment will be carried from this point to the Section bivouacs in the Sunken Road, T.22.d.20.85.

    Guides for No. 2 Section will rendezvous at No. 2 Section Headquarters in the QUARRIES at 5.30 p.m. O.C's Nos. 1 and 2 Sections will arrange to relieve one another as quickly as possible in order that the Limber is not kept waiting at the QUARRY longer than it can possibly be helped. On completion of relief O.C. No. 2 Section will detail 2/Lt. OLNEY with two gun teams to report to Company Headquarters. O.C. No. 2 Section will then take Sergt EDMUNDS and L/c MARR's gun teams to occupy the positions on the outskirts of CROISILLES previously occupied by two guns of No. 3 Section. Map References are as follows :- T.18.c.40.15 & T.17.a.45.55. In order to facilitate these two teams finding the above positions after they have been vacated by No. 3 Section, O.C. No. 2 Section will arrange for one of the Gun Numbers from each team detailed above to reconnoitre the routes to the positions to be taken over some time on the morning of the 15th instant.

3. Rations and water for consumption on the 14th instant will be taken into the line by the relieving Sections. The only rations that will be sent up from Company Headquarters on the night of the 15th instant will be as follows :-

Rations for the two gun teams and Headquarters of No. 2 Section will be sent to their Headquarters in the Sunken Road - T.17.a.70.50 at 7.30 p.m.

Rations for No. 4 Section will be sent to No. 4 Section's new Headquarters in the Sunken Road at T.22.d.10.65 at 10 p.m.

4. Particular attention must be paid to the handing over of all correspondence and firing Schemes issued from this Office in order that the existing schemes may be continued.

5. All belt boxes and tripods will remain in present positions and will be taken over by the relieving Sections. In each case a guard of one man must be provided to remain with them until taken over.
Pte DOWLING will report to O.C. No. 1 Section tomorrow morning and will remain in charge of the tripods and belt boxes of that Section until taken over by No. 4 Section. Tripods and belt boxes at present in possession of the two gun teams at Company Headquarters will be under the charge of the Guard until taken over by No. 2 Section. Tripods and belt boxes of the two guns at CROISILLES will be left in charge of Pte CARR until taken over by No. 2 Section.

6. Relief Complete will be reported direct to Company Headquarters.

7. ACKNOWLEDGE.

(signed)
Lt. & Adjt.
110 Machine Gun Company.

Issued at 5.45 p.m.

Copy No. 1 to O.C. No. 1 Section.
        2   2
        3   3
        4   4
        5 War Diary
        6 War Diary.

APPENDIX '3.

Reference 110th Brigade Operation Orders No. 69
Machine Gun Appendix.

Reference - Sheet 51.b.S.W.4.

Para. 2 of the above Appendix is now cancelled
and the following substituted :-

No. 4 Section of 110 M.G.Company will not be
relieved by No. 1 Section of 62 M.G.Company, but will
continue to occupy the RESERVE LINE North West of
St. LEGER.

No. 1 Section of 62 M.G.Company will take up
positions now being prepared in U.13.c. from which they will
carry out indirect overhead fire during the attack and in
the event of a hostile counter attack.

[signature]
Major,
Commanding,
110 Machine Gun Company.

15/6/17.

SECRET   Copy No. 11

Reference 110th Brigade Operation Orders No. 62.

Machine Gun Appendix.

Reference Sheet 51.b.S.W.4.

1. O.C. 62 Machine Gun Company will arrange for the two and a half Sections referred to in these Operation Orders to move to the Railway Embankment in T.20.d.7.2. by 12 noon on the 15th instant, where accomodation is being arranged.

2. On the afternoon of the 15th instant, No. 1 Section of 62 M.G.Company will relieve No. 4 Section of 110 M.G. Company now occupying the RESERVE LINE North West of St. LEGER.   No. 4 Section of 110 M.G.Company will then move to positions now being prepared in U.13.c.   From here they will carry out indirect overhead fire during the attack and in the event of a hostile counter attack.

3.   No. 4 Section of 62 M.G.Company will move into our present front line on the afternoon of the 15th instant and their four guns will be disposed as follows :-

One gun at U.13.d.75.50 in HUMP AVENUE with lines of fire parallel to the gun of 110 M.G.Company situated at U.13.b.80.20. i.e. down the Valley from THE HUMP to FONTAINE.   This gun will remain here throughout the whole operations and will be used solely in conjunction with the right gun of 110 M.G.Company to put up parallel lines of fire at the bottom of the Valley in the event of a hostile counter attack, but will not fire during the operations.

One gun under cover at Section Headquarters in the M.G.MEBUS situated at U.13.b.35.65.

One gun under cover in the M.G.MEBUS at U.13.b.20.90.

One gun under cover in the M.G.MEBUS at U.7.d.15.20.

The two guns of No. 4 Section 62 M.G.Company detailed for the M.G.MEBUS at U.13.b.35.65, and the M.G.MEBUS at U.7.d.15.20 will proceed after the attack has been reported to have been successful to positions approximately as follows, where the best field of fire can be obtained :-

One gun to position in U.14.a.15.70 to fire down the Valley towards FONTAINE with an alternative line of fire to cover our right flank.

The other gun to a position in U.7.d.65.70 approximately to cover THE SPUR and North of THE SPUR as far as possible towards FONTAINE VILLAGE.

The gun situated at U.13.b.20.90 will be held in Reserve to the two guns up in our new Front Line.

The remaining two guns of No. 2 Section of 62 M.G. Company with the two Reserve guns of 110 M.G.Company will take up positions in T.12.c. where indirect overhead fire will be carried out during the attack and in the event of a hostile counter attack.

Carrying Parties. Three men per gun to be attached to No. 4 Section, 62 M.G.Company, in order to carry 14 belt boxes per gun, two petrol cans of water per gun, 1000 rounds of S.A.A. per gun in bandoliers, one pick and one shovel per gun, four sandbags per man, one Very Light cartridge per man per gun, and one Very Pistol per gun.   Section Officer concerned will check his Section on ZERO day to ensure that these articles are in possession.

Rations for No. 4 Section of 62 M.G.Company will arrive with the rations of Nos. 3 and 1 Sections of 110 M.G. Company at THE QUARRIES at 6 p.m. daily - the necessary ration parties must rendezvous here at this hour.

O.C. No. 62 M.G.Company will arrange to deliver rations to No. 1 Section of 62 M.G.Company direct. Rations for the two guns of No. 2 Section of 62 M.G.Company and the half Section of 110 M.G.Company situated in T.12.c. will be delivered to the Headquarters of No. 2 Section, 110 M.G. Company in the Sunken Road at T.17.a.75.40 at 10.30 p.m. daily - the necessary ration parties must rendezvous here at this hour.

O.C. 62 Machine Gun Company will arrange to send direct to the Q.M.Stores, 110 M.G.Company before 4.30 p.m. daily the necessary rations made up in sandbags and numbered for No. 4 Section 62 M.G.company and the two guns of No. 2 Section 62 M.G.Company not being rationed direct by him. All ration parties should bring an estimated casualty return with them to hand over to the N.C.O. in charge of the limber delivering the rations. Unexpired portion of rations for the 15th and the days rations for the 16th will be carried on the person together with the emergency ration.

Greatcoats and Waterproof Sheets. No. 4 Section of 62 M.G.Company will carry their waterproof sheets. Their greatcoats and packs will be dumped at their Transport Lines before they report to 110 M.G.Company Headquarters at noon on the 15th instant.

ZERO hour will be notified later.

ACKNOWLEDGE.

                                    Major.
                                Commanding,
110 Machine Gun Company.

Issued at   p.m. 14th June 1917.

Copy No. 1 to 110th Infantry Brigade.
      2   O.C. No. 1 Section 62 M.G.Company
      3   2   "   "
      4   4   "   "
      5   1 Section 110 M.G.Company.
      6   2   "   "
      7   3   "   "
      8   4   "   "
      9 Office Copy.
     10 War Diary
     11 War Diary
     12 to O.C. 62 Machine Gun Company.

Sheet 1

110th Machine Gun Company

Army Form C. 2118.

WAR DIARY
INTELLIGENCE SUMMARY
(Erase heading not required.)

Vol 17

Place	Date	Hour	Summary of Events and Information	Remarks and references to Appendices
BLAIRVILLE	1917 July 1st		No 3 Section paraded at 7.30 am, and marched to St LEGER to relieve a Section of the 64th Machine Gun Company occupying the RESERVE line of the RIGHT SECTOR Divisional Front, NORTH of the village.	n.j.B.
			The remainder of the Company paraded at 10 a.m. and marched by Sections to Camp "K" MOYENNEVILLE, relieving the 64th Machine Gun Company in Divisional Reserve.	n.j.B.
MOYENNEVILLE	July 2nd		Situation unaltered.	n.j.B.
"	July 3rd July 8th		Nos 1, 2, and 4 Sections relieved Sections of the 64th Machine Gun Company in the RIGHT SECTOR, Divisional Front. No 3 Section relieved by a Section of the 64th Machine Gun Company, and returned to Company Headquarters, which were now established at the RAILWAY EMBANKMENT T.20.d60.40 (Map Reference 51.B.S.W. 1/20,000)	n.j.B.
			Sections disposed as follows:- Front Line — No 2 Section Support Line — No 4 Section Intermediate Line — No 1 Section Company Headquarters. No 3 Section.	n.j.B.

Army Form C. 2118.

Sheet 2

Instructions regarding War Diaries and Intelligence
Summaries are contained in F. S. Regs., Part II.
and the Staff Manual respectively. Title pages
will be prepared in manuscript.

WAR DIARY

INTELLIGENCE SUMMARY

(Erase heading not required.)

Place	Date	Hour	Summary of Events and Information	Remarks and references to Appendices
ST LEGER	1917 July 9th		Dispositions unaltered, and situation normal. A draft of ten other ranks reported for duty.	App. B.
	"10th to "13th		Dispositions unaltered, and situation normal.	App. B.
-"-	July 14th		Inter. Section relief, after which Sections were disposed as follows:-	
			Front Line — No 4 Section	
			Support Line — No 1 Section	
			Intermediate Line — No 3 Section	
			At Company Head Quarters – No 2 Section.	
			Situation normal.	
-"-	July 15th		Dispositions unaltered, and situation normal.	App. B.
-"-	July 16th			App. B.
-"-	July 17th & July 18th		No 31499, Pte STUNT L. killed at CROISILLES Dispositions unaltered, and situation normal.	App. B. App. B.
-"-	July 20th		Inter. Section relief, after which Sections were disposed as follows:-	

WAR DIARY

INTELLIGENCE SUMMARY

Sheet 3 — Army Form C. 2118.

Place	Date	Hour	Summary of Events and Information	Remarks and references to Appendices
ST LEGER	July 20th	(cont.)	Front Line - No 1 Section. Support Line - No 3 Section. Intermediate Line - No 2 Section. At Company Headquarters - No 4 Section.	
-do-	July 24th July 25th		Dispositions unaltered, and situation normal.	App. B. App. B.
-do-	July 26th		Inter Section relief, after which Sections were disposed as follows:- Front Line - No 3 Section. Support Line - No 2 Section. Intermediate Line - No 4 Section. At Company Headquarters - No 1 Section.	
-do-	July 29th July 30th		Inspection of Transport by the General Officer Commanding the Division. Dispositions unaltered and situation unaltered. —"—	App. B.
	July 31st		Operation orders received for tomorrow's relief	App. B.

SECRET   Copy No. 6

OPERATION ORDERS
by
Lieut T. D. HALLIMAN, Commanding
110 Machine Gun Company.

1. The Company will relieve the 109th Machine Gun Company at "E" Camp, MOYENNEVILLE on July 1st. Relief to be completed by 12 noon.

2. Sections will move off independently with their Section Transport as follows :-
   No. 1 Section at 10 a.m.
   No. 2 Section at 10.5 a.m.
   No. 3 Section at 10.10 a.m.
   No. 4 Section and Headquarters at 10.15 a.m.
   Movement will be by Cross Country Tracks.

3. Sections will halt on the Football Ground in rear of the Camp at MOYENNEVILLE until the latter is vacated by the 109 M.G.Coy.

4. 2/Lt. J.C.KIDD, accompanied by two signallers, will form an advance party, and will move off from present Company H.Q. at 9.30 a.m. The Advance Party will take over the standing accommodation etc of the Camp, giving receipts for same, which will be handed in to the Company Orderly Room on the arrival of the Company.

5. 2/Lt. R.C.KIDD and six men (including the Sanitary Man) will form a rear party and will ensure that the present billets are handed over in a perfectly clean condition. 2/Lt. R.C.KIDD will inspect the Billets etc after the last Section is clear and will render a certificate to the Town Major as to their cleanliness.

6. A Lorry for conveyance of packs will report at Brigade H.Q. BLAIRVILLE at 5 a.m. July 1st. All the packs of the Company must be dumped at the Company Q.M.Stores by 7.30 a.m.

7. The following Transport will report at 5 a.m. at the places mentioned :-
   2 Limbers for Q.M.Stores and Canteen at Q.M.Stores.
   Transport Limber at Transport Lines.
   Water Cart at Transport Lines.
   Headquarters Limber at Officers Mess.
   Mess Cart at Officers Mess.
   As soon as loaded the above will move off together from the Transport Lines accompanied by the Cooks.

8. All Trench Shelters now in possession will be carried.

                                       [signature]
                                       Lt. & Adjt.
                                       110 Machine Gun Company.

Copy No. 1 to O.C. No.1 Section   Copy No.2 to O.C. No. 2 Section
         3   "   " 3   "   4   "   "   " 4   "
         5 to Transport Officer.
         6 War Diary
         7 War Diary.

SECRET   Copy No. 9

OPERATION ORDERS
by
Major A. H. BOWDEN, Commanding
110 Machine Gun Company.

1. The Company will relieve the 64th Machine Gun Company in the Right Sector on July 8th 1917.

2. No. 2 Sectn 110 M.G.Coy will relieve No. 1 Sectn. 64 M.G.Coy.
       4 "   "   "   "   2   "
       1 "   "   "   "   3   "
       3 "   "   " (now in the Reserve Line) will be relieved by No. 4 Section 64 M.G.Coy.

3. After relief, Sections will be disposed as follows :-
       Front Line   No. 2 Section.
       Intermediate Line   No. 4 Section.
       CROISILLES Posts   No. 1 Section.
       Company Headquarters   No. 3 Section.

4. Guides from 64 M.G.Company will rendezvous as follows :-
       One guide per gun for No. 2 Section) At CROISILLES Church
       One guide per gun for No. 4 Section) at 2 p.m.
       Two guides for No. 1 Section at Company Headquarters,
       Railway Embankment at 12.45 p.m.

5. Sections, accompanied by one Gun Limber, will be ready to move off from present area at the following times :-
       No. 2 Section   10.30 a.m.
            4   "   10.45 a.m.
            1   11.   a.m.
   Dinners will be at 12 noon sharp at the New Company Headquarters Railway Embankment, after which, Sections will proceed to relieve in accordance with the times stated in para. 4. The Company Q.M.S. will make the necessary arrangements for the Company Cook to proceed early on the morning of the 8th in order to prepare dinners.

6. The bed of the SENSEE RIVER will be used by all parties by daylight between CROISILLES and the point at which NELLY AVENUE runs into it.

7. The following will be taken over on relief :-
       Belt boxes.
       Trench Stores
       Defence Schemes.
       Maps, Aeroplane photographs etc.
       Trench Shelters.

8. When reporting "Relief Complete" Section Officers will inform Company Headquarters of the number of belt boxes taken over in order that an equal number may be handed over to the 64th Machine Gun Company.

9. The unexpired portion of the days rations for the 8th instant will be carried, also the days rations for the 9th. Rations of Nos. 2 and 4 sections for the 9th will be cooked at Company Headquarters.

10. Rations for all Sections in the line for the 10th instant and onwards will be sent to CROISILLES CHURCH daily to arrive there at 6 p.m. O.C. No. 4 Section will arrange for a party to convey the rations of No. 2 Section to the QUARRY, and O.C. No. 2 Section will arrange for their conveyance from there to his Headquarters.

11. Greatcoats and waterproof sheets will be taken into the line. Packs will be placed on the 'Sections' spare limber before moving off.

12. The two Anti Aircraft mountings at T.22.b.20.00 and T.22.b. 20.20 will be handed over to the relieving Section of the 64th Machine Gun Company.

13. A rough sketch map of the Sector shewing the gun positions is attached hereto.

14. ACKNOWLEDGE.

                                              Lt. & Adjt.
                                    110 Machine Gun Company.

Issued at 3 p.m. 7th July 1917.

        Copy No. 1 to O.C. 64th Machine Gun Company.
               2   O.C. No. 1 Section.
               3   "   2   "
               4   "   3   "
               5   "   4   "
               6   Transport Officer
               7   War Diary
               8   War Diary
               9   Office Copy.

WAR DIARY

~~INTELLIGENCE~~ SUMMARY

Army Form C. 2118.

110th Bay. M.G. Corps Vol 18

Place	Date	Hour	Summary of Events and Information	Remarks and references to Appendices
ST LEGER	1917 Aug 1st		Company relieved in the line by the 64th Machine Gun Company. Section on being relieved marched to Camp "E" MOYENNEVILLE.	
MOYENNEVILLE	Aug 2nd		Company in training	
"	Aug 4th		Company inspected by Brigadier Lord Loch C.M.G., M.V.O., D.S.O.	
"	Aug 5th		Brigade Sports	
"	Aug 8th		Company in training	
"	Aug 9th		Nos 1 and 4 Sections relieved Sections of 64th Machine Gun Company and 237th Machine Gun Company in the line. Nos 2 & 3 Sections relieved the Section of 237th Machine Gun Company in an advanced camp at MOYENNEVILLE, and Company Headquarters were established there.	
"	Aug 10th		Company Headquarters moved to ERVILLERS. The Company were thus disposed as follows:- Company Headquarters, & Nos 2 & 3 Sections at MOYENNEVILLE. Nos 1 and 4 Sections in the line. Transport at ERVILLERS.	
"	Aug 11th to Aug 13th		Situation unaltered.	

Sheet 2.

WAR DIARY
INTELLIGENCE SUMMARY.
(Erase heading not required.)

Army Form C. 2118.

Place	Date	Hour	Summary of Events and Information	Remarks and references to Appendices
MOYENNEVILLE	1918 Aug 4th		Intimation Relief N°s 2 and 3 Sections relieved N°s 1 and 4 Sections in the line. Officially the Company was disposed as follows:— Company Headquarters and N°s 1 and 4 Sections at MOYENNEVILLE. N°s 2 and 3 Sections in the line. Transport at ERVILLERS.	
"	Aug 5th		Situation unaltered.	
"	Aug 6th		Operation Order received from Brigade for tomorrow's relief.	
"	Aug 7th		N°s 2 and 3 Sections relieved by Sections of the 42nd Machine Gun Company. Company returned to rest. Company Camp at MOYENNEVILLE relieving Sections Sections of 62nd Machine Gun Company then Company leaving at MOYENNEVILLE.	
"	Aug 8th to Aug 22nd		Company employed by Brigadier General Kentish C.M.G., M.V.O., D.S.O.	
"	Aug 23rd		Orders Order received for tomorrow's move.	
"	Aug 24th		Company paraded at 8.30 am and marched to ERVILLERS where they entrained for MONCHIET. Transport travelled by MONCHIET by road.	

Sheet 3.

Army Form C. 2118.

WAR DIARY

INTELLIGENCE SUMMARY.

(Erase heading not required.)

Instructions regarding War Diaries and Intelligence Summaries are contained in F. S. Regs., Part II. and the Staff Manual respectively. Title pages will be prepared in manuscript.

Place	Date	Hour	Summary of Events and Information	Remarks and references to Appendices
	1921			
MONCHIET	Aug 26th		The Company paraded at 6.15 p.m. and marched to IZER-LES-HAMEAU where billets were ordered and Company Headquarters established. The Company marched past the Brigadier en route, and the transport were specially commended by him on being the best turned out in the Brigade.	
IZER-LES-HAMEAU	Aug 27th to Aug 31st		Company in training, special attention being given to Passage Drill, and tactical schemes involving its practice.	

Army Form C. 2118.

116 M.G. Coy.

Vol 19

WAR DIARY
or
INTELLIGENCE SUMMARY.
(Erase heading not required.)

Place	Date	Hour	Summary of Events and Information	Remarks and references to Appendices
IZEL-LEZ-HAMEAU	1917 Sept 1st to 5th		Company in training at IZEL LEZ HAMEAU	
	6th 7th 8th		Orders received for O.C. and half the Company to hold themselves in readiness to move. O.C. and half the personnel of the Company entrained at 10.15 a.m. and proceeded to No 2 Camp DICKEBUSCH via St POL and HAZEBROUCK arriving there at 8.30 p.m.	
DICKEBUSCH	9th to 16th		Half the Company at DICKEBUSCH were attached to 39th Division and were engaged in the work of preparing M.G. Emplacements at SHREWSBURY FOREST East of YPRES. The other half of the Company continued their training at IZEL LEZ HAMEAU	
IZEL LEZ HAMEAU	17th		The Left Company from IZEL LEZ HAMEAU joined the Right Company at Camp 2 DICKEBUSCH.	
DICKEBUSCH	18th		The Company proceeded to the line occupying the positions prepared at SHREWSBURY	
	19th 20th		Company in the line. The Company co-operated in the attack of the 39th Divsn with M.G. Barrage Fire.	

Army Form C. 2118.

WAR DIARY
INTELLIGENCE SUMMARY.
(Erase heading not required.)

Instructions regarding War Diaries and Intelligence Summaries are contained in F.S. Regs., Part II and the Staff Manual respectively. Title pages will be prepared in manuscript.

2/

Place	Date	Hour	Summary of Events and Information	Remarks and references to Appendices
	1917			
DICKEBUSCH	Sept 21st		Company in the line	
	22nd		The Company were relieved and proceeded to Camp 2 DICKEBUSCH	
	23rd		Company marched to METEREN where they regained 2nd Division	
METEREN	24th to 28th		Company encamped at METEREN.	
	29th		Company paraded at 10.15 am and marched to MICMAC CAMP.	
MICMAC CAMP	29th		Company paraded at 9.30 am and marched to RIDGE WOOD - S.W. of YPRES.	
RIDGE WOOD	30		Company encamped at RIDGE WOOD.	

Appendices

A Operation Orders of 20th Sept.
B Casualties
C Report on Operations

Appendix "A"

SECRET   Copy No. 1

110th MACHINE GUN COMPANY OPERATION ORDER No. 11

Reference 1/10,000 SHREWSBURY FOREST SHEET, and other Maps issued.

In continuation of 39th Division Operation Order No. 153, already communicated to those concerned, the 110th, 238th and half of 116th Machine Gun Companies will co-operate during the operations with overhead Machine Gun Barrage fire. The 110th Machine Gun Company will constitute Group 1 which will be organised and administered according to the attached detailed orders issued as Appendices "A" and "B".

ACKNOWLEDGE.

18.9.17   2/Lt. & Adjt.
            110 Machine Gun Company.

Copies issued at 10 p.m. to :-

  No. 1 - War Diary
    2 - War Diary
    3 - 117th Brigade Headquarters.
    4 - D.M.G.O. 39th Division.
    5 - D.M.G.O. 21st Division.
    6 - O.C. "A" Battery
    7 - O.C. "B" Battery
    8 - O.C. No. 1 Section
    9 - O.C. No. 2 Section.
   10 - O.C. No. 3 Section.
   11 - O.C. No. 4 Section.
   12 - Office Copy.

MACHINE GUNS.

TABLE "A".

GROUP 1.

Battery.	Location.	Targets.	Firing From	Firing To.	Rate of fire per gun.	Remarks.
A	I.36.b.50.82	J.32.b.45.00 – J.32.b.70.90.	(0 (+10	+10' +35'	1 belt in 4 mins. 1 belt in 2 mins.	
		J.33.a.50.00 – J.33.a.45.00.	(+1 hr 35' (+1 hr 28' (+1 hr 52'	+1 hr 28' +1 hr 52' +4 hrs 13'	1 belt in 6 mins. 1 belt in 4 mins. 1 belt in 10 mins.	(Only 2 guns per Section will fire during this period unless otherwise ordered by Div.H.Q.
			(+4 hrs 13' (+4 hrs 35'	+4hrs 35' +4hrs 55'	1 belt in 4 mins. 1 belt in 10 mins.	
B	I.36.b.50.90.	J.32.b.70.75 – J.27.o.00.65.	(0 (+10	+10' +35'	1 belt in 4 mins. 1 belt in 2 mins.	
		J.33.a.50.70 – J.27.o.45.60.	(+1 hr 35' (+1 hr 28' (+1 hr 52'	+1 hr 28' +1 hr 52' +4hrs 13'	1 belt in 6 mins. 1 belt in 4 mins. 1 belt in 10 mins.	(Only 2 guns per Section will fire during this period unless otherwise ordered by Div.H.Q.
			(+4 hrs 13' (+4 hrs 35'	+4hrs 35' +4hrs 55'	1 belt in 4 mins. 1 belt in 10 mins.	

DETAILED ORDERS 110th MACHINE GUN COMPANY

APPENDIX "A"

The 110th Machine Gun Company will constitute Group No. 1 which will be organised as follows :-

Group	Bty	Battery composition	Battery Commander	Battery officers	Group commander	Battery H.Q.	Group F.O.	Location directing gun	1st Location of ammunition	Reserve	Repair shop
1	A	4 men per gun Nos.1 & 2 Sectns 2 S'ctn Sergts 1 Sig-naller	~~~~ ~~~~ Lieut Overend	~~~ ~~~ B/Lt Clancy	Major Boyden 2nd Lt Creas-Lock 2nd Lt Bambury 2nd Lt Runnan	L.33.b. 32.77	~~~ ~~~ ~~~ Cahal Transit Station Aug-out 1367 30.95	L.33.b. 32.77	150,000 S.A.A 1.55.b. 33.77	20000 S.A.A T.33. b.50. 80.	25 N.C. Dug-out T.29.D. 83.50
1	B	4 men per gun Nos. 3 & 4 Sectns 2 Sectn Sergts 1 Sig-naller	Lieut Sub-char	~~ ~~ B/Lt Ahern		L.33.b 31.87		L.33.a 31.87	150,000 S.A.A 1.33.b 31.87		

ARTILLERY "X" (Contd)

ASSEMBLY POSITION

The personnel of the 110th Machine Gun Company will move to their battle position on C/D Night under orders to be issued later.
ROUTE :- LA CLYTTE - PALLERAST CORNER - CONNAUGHT SOUTH -
(I.16.b.O.4) RIDGE WOOD ROAD thence over and track to TRAGEDY
HUT NO - SPOIL BANK - ROUTE "G" via the DUMP - REINFORCE TO
I.33,b,92,97.

PRELIMINARIES AND WORK

During C and D Day Battery Commanders will lay out all the lines of
fire ready to pin their card and F to the posts immediately
after dusk on D/E night. Work in the trench will be continued
until 2330 - S hours, when batteries will make all preparations
for action.
Machine guns will be placed not more than 10 yards apart to
economise space and facilitate control. The danger zone
immediately in front of each battery position will be fenced with
wire to prevent runners, wounded, and stragglers getting into
the line of fire.

BARRAGE LINES

At ZERO on E day (hour to be notified later) batteries will
commence firing in accordance with Table "A", Fire Organisation
Orders and Maps attached (these only issued to those concerned)
Special care must be taken to ensure that all guns conform to
the rate of fire and time periods detailed.

S.O.S. *After the 14th inst, the S.O.S. Signal will be :- RED, over GREEN, over YELLOW*

In the event of the S.O.S. Signal being received after operations
all machine guns will open on their final barrage lines at the
rate of one belt per gun in two minutes for ten minutes, and
thereafter 50 rounds a minute until the situation is clear.

COMMUNICATIONS

Group Headquarters Group Headquarters will be in direct
telephone communication with D.M.G.O. AT LARCH WOOD by buried
cable. Each Battery will be in communication with Group
Headquarters by buried or armoured cable as circumstances admit.
Battery Commanders must be in close touch with the telephone
throughout the operations. Should they have to leave, a
reliable N.C.O. or man must always be detailed to answer for
them.

RUNNERS

Battery Commanders will each detail four runners to report to
Group Headquarters after sundown in their battery positions
on C/D night. One from each battery will be kept at Group
Headquarters. The others will be returned.

DANGER ZONE

Battery Commanders will arrange for the wire protecting the
danger zone of their battery to be inspected periodically, and a
look out man should be posted to give warning to any wounded or
stragglers who may be approaching the wire.

REPAIR DEPOT

A Repair Shop will be established at R.E Machine Gun Dugout at
I.33.c.83.50 from "D" Day. All Battery Commanders will make
themselves acquainted with the position of this dugout.

HOSTILE AIRCRAFT

Arrangements have been made for at least four guns in the vicinity of the Battery Positions to engage hostile aircraft within range. Should however any enemy aircraft manoeuvre at low range immediately over our battery positions, one gun per battery will be prepared to engage same. Whenever the guns are not actually firing Battery Commanders will ensure that the camouflage nets provided are invariably kept in position over the guns.

BELT FILLING

Battery Commanders will arrange a definite system of belt filling for each pair of guns in order to cope with the rate of fire of all guns: this system must be very carefully organised.

CONCEALMENT

In order to ensure that the concentration of troops is not given away to low flying aeroplanes, all troops will be kept under cover during "D" day as far as possible.

APPENDIX "B"
ADMINISTRATION

RATIONS

Rations for "D" and "E" days will be carried. Subsequently, rations will be delivered to Battery Positions daily under arrangements to be made by Transport Officer. Further details regarding time etc will be notified direct.

MEDICAL ARRANGEMENTS

A Divisional Collecting Station has been established at 1.29.d.30.30.

KIT

All packs will be dumped in the Headquarters Stores before leaving Camp on "C"/"D" Night.

Battery Commanders will ensure that the following equipment is taken into action :-

Guns, Tripods, Spare Parts, Condensers, Petrol Cans.
14 belt boxes per gun.
2 belt filling machines per Section.
2 petrol cans per gun for drinking water
2 petrol cans per gun for cooling water.
1 can of lubricating oil per Section.
2 barrels per gun.
1 "T" and ZERO aiming post per gun.
2 Clinometers per Section.
1 Spirit level per gun.
Rations for "D" and "E" days.
Greatcoats may be carried if required.
1 telephone per Section with ¼ mile of wire.
2 telephones at Group Headquarters with ½ mile of
                                            wire.
Battery Organisation Charts and Barrage Charts.
1 Stretcher per Battery.
Tommies Cookers.

DUMPS ETC.

See attached Group Organisation Sheet.

Appendix B

CASUALTIES
sustained by 110th Machine Gun Company
during period 18th Septr - 22nd Sept 1917.

	2/Lt.	Olney J.K.	Wounded	20.9.17	H.E.	
37287	Pte	Holding W.	"	18.9.17	"	
7088		Swan W.	"	"	"	
5805		Hennesey J.	Killed	20.9.17	"	
45821		Archer S.	"	"	"	
60072		Jackson P.	"	"	"	
45679		Cummins G.	"	22.9.17	"	
5848	L/c	Farquhar W.	Wounded	20.9.17	"	
51452	Pte	Amos H.	"	"	"	
64179		Rice B.	"	"	"	
90455		Doble H.T.	"	"	"	
33051		McVeigh G.	"	"	"	
15943		Druce H.	"	"	"	
31829	L/c	McLean W.	"	"	"	
8215	Pte	Bird A.	"	"	"	
45911	L/c	Boyle W.	"	"	"	
5829	Pte	Corps J.W.	"	"	"	
10354		Malin R.	"	"	"	
5861		Ingram J.	"	"	"	
67946		Summerhill S.	"	"	"	
62981		Hill S.O.	"	"	"	
73606		Ball W.	"	"	"	
83815		Daniels T.	"	"	"	
25157		Moore W.	Shock, Shell	"	"	Since Returned
45908	L/c	Kinsella M.	"	"	"	
19001	Pte	Williams W.	"	"	"	
24549		Kelly P.	Gas, Mustard	18.9.17	"	
53227		Wells A.	"	"	"	
29649		Jackson P.	"	"	"	
5898	Cpl	Prescott H.	Wounded	22.9.17	H.E.	
14841	Pte	Munson R.A.	"	"	"	

Appendix C

Report on the action of
110th Machine Gun Company whilst
attached to the 39th Division for
operations on September 20th.

The first week of the time during which the 110th Machine Gun Company was attached to the 39th Division was occupied in constructing dugouts, emplacements, Belt Filling Depots etc. in the vicinity of SHREWSBURY FOREST.

The services of 6 R.E. were obtained, and, with their assistance, we were enabled to sink 50 feet of shafting in the trench which eventually proved to be ample cover for the Batteries.

On the night before the attack (Sept. 18/19th) everything was in readiness, all materials and gun equipment had been carried up, and the Batteries moved ibto position, leaving Company Headquarters at 1 a.m.).

On the evening of Sept. 19th Group Headquarters were established at the Central Visual Station, 50 yards in rear of Batteries) and everything was in readiness for the attack.

At 6.40 a.m. on September 20th the Artillery and Machine Gun Barrages opened simultaneously, and the German barrage was put down a few minutes later.

During the remainder of the morning and throughout the afternoon, the Batteries and Group Headquarters were intermittently shelled by 5.9's and several casualties were sustained.

Later in the day news was received that the Division on our left had not attained their final objective and would attack the GREEN LINE at 6.19 p.m. The Group co-operated with Groups 2 and 2 A. assisting the attack with barrage fire.

At 6.49 p.m. all guns ceased fire and lay on their S.O.S. lines ready to fire in the event of receiving the S.O.S.Signal.

Nothing further of note occurred during the night beyond the continued shelling of the Batteries and Group Headquarters.

On September 21st at 4.30 a.m. half the Group co-operated with the Artillery in putting down a precautionary barrage vertically searching 100 yards and coming back to the S.O.S. line.

At 9 a.m. the enemy were observed in large parties on the ground in rear of JOIST TRENCH and the S.E. side of the Hill in front of GHELUVERT leading up to JOIST TRENCH. A number of the enemy were also seen entering the dugouts in the vicinity of ALASKA HOUSE. Both Batteries fired on "B" Battery S.O.S. Lines and fired at the rate of one belt in three minutes until 9.25 a.m.

At 9.25 a.m. all guns were laid according to instructions issued from the D.M.G.O.

At 10 a.m. the enemy were observed to be moving in the same neighbourhood in parties of about 20, and were promptly engaged.

Nothing further was observed until 12.15 p.m. when enemy movement was again noticed in the neighbourhood of JOIST TRENCH and our fire was brought to bear upon the parties.

At 12. 29 p.m. the enemy were again observed here in large parties. Both Batteries fired two belts rapid. Visibility at this time was excellent, and the enemy were observed to run to cover in all directions. The enemy retaliated slightly with shell fire in the vicinity of the Batteries. Throughout the afternoon the enemy were observed to be still moving very cautiously in the same neighbourhood, our fire harassing them continuously. 228th Machine Gun Company were informed of the movement and fired at a slow rate on their S.O.S. lines.

At 7.1 p.m. the enemy launched his counter attack. All guns were in readiness and opened up immediately on receipt of the S.O.S. Signal. Throughout the night the enemy shelled heavily with 5.9's and gas shells, but caused no damage, the men being on the alert for gas.

On September 22nd preparations were made to with--draw the Group. Just prior to withdrawing however the enemy shelled the Batteries and Group Head--quarters heavily, inflicting several casualties. The shelling subsided slightly at 11 a.m. and the Company left the position and returned to Company Headquarters.

A list of the casualties sustained by the Company during the whole period it was attached to the 39th Division is attached.

During the operations chronicled above, several lessons, both tectical and technical were brought out which are undoubtedly of considerable importance. These are attached hereto.

24.9.17.

Tactical and Technical lessons
learnt during Operations of 20/9/17.

TACTICAL

1. The importance of maintaining a liason between the Artillery F.O.O. and the Machine Gun Group Commander. This was especially emphasised during the recent operations when this Company was attached to your Division. The very closest liason was established with the F.O.O. throughout, and consequently every target that presented itself was dealt with in a very gratifying manner.

2. That Machine Gun Companies should move complete instead of half personnel being sent forward in advance to prepare emplacements etc. It was found that a half Company was insufficient to carry out the work of constructing dugouts, emplacements etc in preparation for the attack of your Division, and entailed a severe strain upon the half Company so employed.

3. <u>Medical Arrangements</u> Owing to the isolated position of the Group during the recent operations, arrangements were made for a Senior N.C.O. to render First Aid. This arrangement proved to be perfectly satisfactory and was absolutely essential in order to dress the wounded and render First Aid generally.

TECHNICAL

Belt filling machines were found to be absolutely useless. During the recent operations, when the guns fired a total of 360,000 rounds, every endeavour was made to facilitate the use of the Belt Filling Machine by means of strong tables which were made and fixed firmly into the ground in each belt filling Depot, but even the men most experienced in their use found it quicker to fill belts by hand.

The ammunition used throughout the whole of these operations was "K.16" and 360,000 were fired in all and the ammunition was found to be entirely satisfactory in every way.

Throughout the operations all telephonic communications were out of action due to shell fire. Group and Brigade Headquarters were only in communication intermittently during "E" and "F" days. In view of the above I think that if a map could be supplied to the Group Commander showing all communications leading back from his Group Headquarters via the different signal stations he would then be able to ensure that every effort was being made at his own end to regain telephonic communication with the Brigade Head- quarters to whom he is attached.

WAR DIARY

INTELLIGENCE SUMMARY

Sheet 1
Army Form C. 2118.

11th M.G. Coy

Place	Date	Hour	Summary of Events and Information	Remarks and references to Appendices
RIDGE WOOD CAMP nr. DICKEBUSCH	Oct 1st 1917	—	Company Headquarters established at RIDGE WOOD CAMP. Working parties engaged in constructing emplacements and digging shelters at POLYGON WOOD in preparation for the forthcoming operations.	
—	Oct 2nd	5.30pm	The two Batteries, consisting of eight guns per Battery, moved off from Company Headquarters to take up their positions at POLYGON WOOD. They moved by Sections at 200 yards interval with their gun equipment on pack animals, and N°1 accompanied his own gun with the mule driver and following in rear of his own Section. No casualties whatever were sustained en route. During the occupation of the Pill-box, and in carrying spare guns, equipment and ammunition from the Company dump, the first casualties were sustained. Of the 3rd O.R. attached from the Leicestershire Regt for carrying purposes, only one was now left, the remainder having either been great or wounded.	
POLYGON WOOD	Oct 3rd 1917		Throughout this morning, the situation was comparatively quiet in the vicinity of the Battery position, but at 2.30 p.m. and 3.15 p.m. an artillery carried out test barrages, which provoked retaliation, and the Batteries were	

Army Form C. 2118.

Sheet 2.

WAR DIARY
or
INTELLIGENCE SUMMARY

(Erase heading not required.)

Instructions regarding War Diaries and Intelligence Summaries are contained in F. S. Regs., Part II. and the Staff Manual respectively. Title pages will be prepared in manuscript.

Place	Date	Hour	Summary of Events and Information	Remarks and references to Appendices
POLYGON WOOD	Oct 3rd 1917 (contd)		heavily shelled. The enemy shelling continued throughout the night, becoming intense towards ZERO hour	
"	Oct 4th	6 a.m.	At 6 a.m. our Artillery barrage opened, and three minutes later, our Machine Gun barrage co-operated. The guns fired until 9.20 a.m.	Appendix "A" 6.9.08/12
		9 a.m.	At this hour "B" Battery had only one gun in action, the remainder having either been buried or destroyed by shell fire. Information concerning the general situation could not be obtained, owing to all communications having been cut by the shelling, and messages could only be got through by means of runners.	
		3.30 p.m.	Heavy shelling continued, and at 5.30 p.m. the enemy launched his counter-attack. The incoming gun fire on their S.O.S. lines immediately on receipt of the signal. The counter attack was unsuccessful, but the heavy shelling in the vicinity of the Batteries continued until 8 p.m.	
		8 p.m.	Situation became abnormally quiet.	
"	Oct 5th 1917	2.30 am	Orders received to withdraw to Company Transport Lines	
"	"	6.0 am	Withdrawal completed without further casualties. A hot meal and tea was provided for the men, after which they turned in and slept throughout the day	

WAR DIARY

INTELLIGENCE SUMMARY.

(Erase heading not required.)

Army Form C. 2118.

Sheet 3

Place	Date	Hour	Summary of Events and Information	Remarks and references to Appendices
RIDGE WOOD CAMP	Oct 5th 1917	9 a.m.	The Company cleaned guns and equipment, checked kits &c., also cleaned up themselves.	
"	"	3 p.m.	Orders received to put 14 guns in the line. Ten of these guns were to take over forward positions from 6th, 61st, 63rd, and 234th Machine Gun Companies, and four were to assist the Barrage Battery at J 9 d 90.20 (Ypres Sheet 28 10,000) of the C.S.M. of 62nd Machine Gun Company,	
POLYGON WOOD	"	8 p.m.	Company moved off guided by the C.S.M. of 62nd Machine Gun Company, and had great difficulty in reaching CHATEAU WOOD owing to a very bad track. The fourteen guns, three tripods, water and rations were in great demand from CHATEAU WOOD onwards to J 9 d 90.20. The party was continuously shelled, and several mules killed with the rations and guns, and could not be found. Only seven guns arrived at the Battery position. Guides were waiting there for the ten forward guns	
"	"	12.30 a.m.	The Relief started. The Company took over tripods and belt boxes at all gun positions except at one position where there were no tripods.	
"	"	2.0 a.m.	Relief completed reported. The report was delayed owing to the runners getting lost on their way to Company Headquarters	

Sheet 4

Army Form C. 2118.

WAR DIARY
INTELLIGENCE SUMMARY.
(Erase heading not required.)

Place	Date	Hour	Summary of Events and Information	Remarks and references to Appendices
POLYGON WOOD	Oct 7th 1917		Continued shelling. A good supply of rations & water was sent up during the night to relieve those lost on the way up. The forward guns were unable to fire more than a few belts as immediately they opened fire, they were located and shelled. Orderlies were maintained at the "BUTTE" and CHATEAU WOOD and a relay post at HELL FIRE CORNER in co-operation with "B" Battalion at RIDGE WOOD CAMP. This system of communication was found to be invaluable throughout the operations.	
-"-	Oct 8th 1917		Nothing of importance occurred except that there was fairly heavy shelling. In the evening of this day, as no orders had been received regarding the barrage guns, they were laid on "the BUTTE" ready for a ZERO order when orders should arrive.	
		11.30 p.m.	Lieut. CHITTENDEN of 231st Machine Gun Company arrived and said that he had received a verbal message re ZERO time. Runners were then sent out to all forward guns giving them the time.	
-"-	Oct 9th 1917		A few forward guns engaged during the day with excellent results. Two of the forward guns were knocked out each time a barrage was put down, and on P. Kenn	

Sheet 5

Army Form C. 2118.

WAR DIARY
or
INTELLIGENCE SUMMARY.
(Erase heading not required.)

Place	Date	Hour	Summary of Events and Information	Remarks and references to Appendices
POLYGON WOOD	Oct 9th 1917 (cont)		was completely destroyed. 2/Lieut OLLEY was wounded on this date. Two guns at J10c 20.30 fired on the POEZELHOEK RIDGE from ZERO plus 3 to ZERO plus 28. Two guns at J10c 45.45 fired on the BECELAERE RIDGE from ZERO plus 3 to ZERO plus 28.	W.B.
-"-	Oct 10th 1917		Situation quiet during the morning.	W.B.
		3.30pm	Orders received to withdraw all guns except four at J10c 20.30, J10c 15.35, J11c 20.30 and J11c 10.50 which were to be relieved by 220th Machine Gun Coy. Guides were provided and the relief carried out.	W.B.
-"-	Oct 11th 1917	12 noon	Company paraded and marched to OUDERDOM, entraining there at 5.6pm. Detrained at EBBLINGHEM at 9.45 p.m. and marched to billets at WARDRECQUES.	W.B. W.B.
WARDRECQUES	Oct 12th to Oct 18th 1917		Company in training at WARDRECQUES.	W.B.
-"-	Oct 19th 1917		Orders received to move to DICKEBUSCH area.	W.B.
-"-	Oct 20th 1917	3.45pm	Company paraded and marched to EBBLINGHEM, where it entrained for DICKEBUSCH.	W.B.

Army Form C. 2118.

Sheet 6

WAR DIARY
INTELLIGENCE SUMMARY.
(Erase heading not required.)

Place	Date	Hour	Summary of Events and Information	Remarks and references to Appendices
DICKEBUSCH	Oct 21st 1917	2 a.m.	Detrained at DICKEBUSCH and marched to billets	
-"-	Oct 22nd 1917		Company in billets cleaning up generally. Bombs were dropped by hostile aircraft but no casualties resulted.	
-"-	Oct 23rd 1917	12.30 p.m.	Company paraded and marched to the CHATEAU SEGARD where it encamped.	
CHATEAU SEGARD	Oct 28th 1917		Company encamped. Area bombing by hostile aircraft, but no casualties inflicted	
POLYGON WOOD	Oct 29th 1917	4.30 a.m.	Company paraded and moved into the line, taking up positions in the vicinity of POLYGON WOOD.	
-"-	Oct 29th to Oct 31st		Company in the line.	

APPENDIX "A"

SECRET   Copy No. 2

110th MACHINE GUN COMPANY OPERATION ORDER No. 12.

Reference 1/10,000 BECELAERE Sheet.

In continuation of 110th Machine Gun Company
Warning Order No. 12, already communicated to
those concerned, 16 guns of 110th, 8 guns of 62nd,
8 guns of 64th, and 12 guns of 237th Machine Gun
Companies will co-operate during the operations
with overhead Machine Gun Barrage Fire.
The 110th Machine Gun Company will constitute
Group No. 1 which will be organised and admin-
-istered according to the attached detailed
orders issued as Appendices.

ACKNOWLEDGE

                                   DB Barclay 2/
                                        Lt. & Adjt.
                                   110 Machine Gun Company.

Issued at 6.30 p.m.

Copy No. 1 - War Diary
        2 - War Diary
        3 - ~~110th Brigade Headquarters~~ TRANSPORT OFFICER
        4 - D.M.G.O., 21st Division.
        5 - O.C. "A" Battery
        6 - O.C. "B" Battery
        7 - O.C. No. 1 Section.
        8 - O.C. No. 2 Section.
        9 - O.C. No. 3 Section.
       10 - O.C. No. 4 Section.
       11 - Office Copy.

Detailed Orders — 110th Machine Gun Company

Appendix "A"

The 110th Machine Gun Company will constitute Group No 1 which will be organised as follows:—

Group	Battery	Fighting Personnel	Battery Commander	Battery Officer	Group Commander	Battery HQ	Group HQ	Location of Director Gun
1	A	4 men per gun Nos 1–2 Sections 2 Section Sergts 1 Signaller	Lieut Hitchens	Lieut Ainscough	Major Bowden 1 Signaller	T.9.c.74.30	T.9.c.60.30	T.9.c.74.30
1	B	4 men per gun Nos 3–4 Sections 2 Section Sergts 1 Signaller	Lieut Fanning	2/Lieut R.G. Kidd		T.9.c.78.40		T.9.c.78.40

APPENDIX "A"

The personnel of the 110th Machine Gun Company will move to its battle position on night October 2nd/3rd under orders to be issued later.
One Officer and one Guide will accompany every four guns.
Routes as already detailed.

TRANSPORT
As many journeys as may be necessary will be made by the pack mules after taking their first load of guns etc to Group Headquarters on the night of October 2nd/3rd in order to transfer the remainder of S.A.A. and water at present on the Dump to the Battery Positions. One senior N.C.O. will be stationed at the S.A.A. dump until the last load has been transferred, when he will report to Group Headquarters, and Lieut BUTCHER will return with the Train to Company Headquarters.
N.B. Should the pack mules be unable to carry out the work detailed above before dawn Oct. 3rd, they will report to the S.A.A. dump again at 9 p.m. October 3rd.

FIRE DIRECTION AND WORK
During Zero - 1 day, Battery Commanders will lay out all the lines of fire and fix their ZERO and T aiming posts. Work in the positions will be continued until ZERO - 2 hours when Batteries will make all preparations for action.
Barrage guns will be placed not more than 10 yards apart to economise space and facilitate control. The danger zone immediately in front of each Battery position will be fenced with signal wire where necessary to prevent runners, wounded and stragglers getting into the line of fire.
No. 1's will be continually on the look out for any of these who may wander across the danger zone.

FIRE ORDERS
At ZERO hour (to be notified later) Batteries will commence firing in accordance with Table "A", Fire Organisation Orders and Maps (Maps only issued to those concerned)
Special care must be taken to ensure that all guns conform to the rate of fire and time periods detailed
The S.O.S. signal will in all probability be as follows :-
    S.O.S. by night - RED over GREEN over YELLOW
    S.O.S. by day - RED smoke.
Should any alteration be received from Division it will be immediately notified to Battery Commanders. In the event of the S.O.S. Signal being received after operations, all Machine Guns will open on their final barrage lines at the rate of one belt per gun in two minutes for ten minutes and thereafter 20 rounds a minute until the situation is clear.

COMMUNICATIONS
Telephonic Communication will be established in accordance with the Plan of Communications already issued to those concerned with Instructions No. 1.

BELT FILLING

Battery Commanders will arrange a definite system of belt filling for each pair of guns in order to cope with the rate of fire of all guns. This system must be very carefully organised.

CONCEALMENT

In order to ensure that the concentration of troops is not given away to low flying aeroplanes, all troops will be kept under cover during ZERO - 1 day.

HOSTILE AIRCRAFT

One gun per Battery will be detailed to engage low flying aeroplanes, and for this purpose will be provided with special Anti Aircraft mountings.

SYNCHRONIZATION

Watches will be synchronized at Group Headquarters at 6 p.m. on ZERO - 1 day, and at three hours before ZERO.

APPENDIX "B"

RATIONS

Rations for ZERO - 1 and ZERO days will be carried. Subsequently, rations will be delivered by pack mules to Group Headquarters, arriving there at approximately 11 p.m. nightly.

MEDICAL ARRANGEMENTS

One R.A.M.C. Orderly will be attached to each Battery for rendering First Aid, and will accompany the Batteries into the line on night of October 2nd/3rd.
Other Medical Arrangements have already been notified.

KIT

All packs will be dumped in Headquarters Stores before leaving on night of 2nd/3rd October.

Battery Commanders will ensure that the following equipment is taken into action :-
Guns, Tripods, Condensers or Petrol Cans.
1 First Aid Case per two guns
1 Spare Parts Box per Battery
All Belt Boxes
2 Petrol Cans per gun for cooling water
2 Petrol Cans per gun for drinking water
1 Can of Lubricating Oil per Section
2 Barrels per gun
One "T" and ZERO aiming Post per gun
2 Clinometers per Section.
1 Spirit level per gun
Rations for ZERO - 1 and ZERO days.
~~Greatcoats may be carried if required.~~
Battery Organisation Charts and Barrage Charts
1 telephone per Section with ¼ mile of wire
2 Telephones at Group Headquarters with ½ mile of wire.
Three Stretchers.
Tommies Cookers
1 Spare Parts Box for Group Headquarters.

Vol 21

ORIGINAL

WAR

— OF —

DIARY

110TH MACHINE GUN COMPANY

1ST to 30TH NOVEMBER 1917.

Vol 22.

Army Form C. 2118.

WAR DIARY
INTELLIGENCE SUMMARY.
(Erase heading not required.)

Sheet I

Place	Date	Hour	Summary of Events and Information	Remarks and references to Appendices
POLYGON WOOD	1917 Nov. 1st to 4th		Company in the line	W.A
"	5th		Company relieved by 62nd Machine Gun Company and marched to Divl Headquarters at CHATEAU SEGARD	W.A
CHATEAU SEGARD	6th to 15th		Company in Camp at CHATEAU SEGARD – cleaning up generally and training. Bombs were dropped by hostile aircraft during this time, but no casualties inflicted. Orders received that Company were being transferred to First Army by march route	W.A
"	16th	9am	Company paraded and marched to Camp No. 11 at RENINGHELST	W.A
RENINGHELST	17th		At Camp No. 11. Day spent in cleaning up generally	
"	18th		Company marched to DOULIEU and billeted there for the night	
DOULIEU	19th		" " " LA COURONNE	
LA COURONNE	20th		" " " VENDIN LEZ BETHUNE	
VENDIN-LEZ-BETHUNE	21st		" " " HERSIN COUPIGNY	
HERSIN COUPIGNY	22nd to 24th		In billets at HERSIN COUPIGNY. – Time devoted to cleaning up and training. Whilst here the town was bombarded by hostile artillery for no casualties were inflicted on this Company	W.A

WAR DIARY
INTELLIGENCE SUMMARY. Sheet II

Army Form C. 2118.

Place	Date	Hour	Summary of Events and Information	Remarks and references to Appendices
HERSIN	1917 Nov 25	9.30 a.m.	Company paraded and marched to Lillers at HOUVELIN	
HOUVELIN	26th to 29th		Company at HOUVELIN. Time devoted to cleaning up, checking gun parts and equipment, kit inspection, and training generally.	
			Orders received that the Royals would move to the CHELERS area.	
- " -	30th	5 p.m.	Orders received that the Transport would march to ARRAS tonight and Company entrain the next day.	
		6.30 p.m.	Orders received that the Company would entrain at SAVY at 8 p.m. Company paraded at 7 p.m. and entrained at SAVY - eight limbers detraining with the Company and the rest of the transport marching by road.	

Vol 22

ORIGINAL

W A R

D I A R Y

- of -

110th MACHINE GUN COMPANY for

DECEMBER 1917.

Vol. 23

Army Form C. 2118.

WAR DIARY
INTELLIGENCE SUMMARY.
(Erase heading not required.)

Instructions regarding War Diaries and Intelligence Summaries are contained in F. S. Regs., Part II. and the Staff Manual respectively. Title pages will be prepared in manuscript.

Place	Date	Hour	Summary of Events and Information	Remarks and references to Appendices
	1917 Decr 1st		Detrained at TINCOURT at 10 a.m. and marched to Billets there. Orders received for Company to take over positions in the Line tomorrow.	
TINCOURT	2nd		Company marched into the Line and took over positions. Company Headquarters and Transport at MARQUAIX.	
EPEHY	3rd to 5th		Company in the Line. Headquarters and Transport at MARQUAIX.	
"	6th		Headquarters and Transport moved to VILLERS FAUCON.	
"	7th) 8th)		Situation unchanged.	
"	9th		Company relieved by the 237th Machine Gun Company with the exception of four guns. Sections on being relieved marching to Billets at LONGAVESNES.	
LONGAVESNES	10th to 16th		Company in Divisional Reserve at LONGAVESNES. Time devoted to cleaning up, kit inspections checking spare parts, training etc.	
"	17th		Relieved 237th Machine Gun Company in the line. Headquarters and Transport at VILLERS FAUCON.	
EPEHY	18th 19th		Company in the Line. - do - Bomb dropped on Company Headquarters in the Line by hostile aircraft, wounding C.O. two other Officers, two Other Ranks, and one attached R.A.M.C. man. List attached marked "A".	
"	20th to 25th		Company in the line. Situation normal.	
"	26th		Company, with the exception of four guns, relieved by 237th Machine Gun Company. Sections on being relieved marching to billets at LONGAVESNES.	

Army Form C. 2118.

WAR DIARY
~~INTELLIGENCE SUMMARY.~~
(Erase heading not required.)

Instructions regarding War Diaries and Intelligence Summaries are contained in F. S. Regs., Part II. and the Staff Manual respectively. Title pages will be prepared in manuscript.

Place	Date	Hour	Summary of Events and Information	Remarks and references to Appendices
LONGAVESNES	27th		Company in Divisional Reserve.	
"	28th		Situation unchanged.	
"	29th		Inter Section relief of the four guns in the Line.	
"	30th		Situation unchanged.	
"	31st		Guns in the line relieved by the 1st M.M.G.Battery.	

Appendix "A"

110th Machine Gun Company

CASUALTIES sustained on Decr 19th by Bomb dropped from hostile aircraft.

Capt. T. D. Hallinan.   C.O.

Lieut A. G. Butcher

Lieut J. Whitehead

No. 5898 Sgt Prescott H.

No. 8850 Pte Rose J. (Remained at duty)

No. 339402 Pte J.B.Booth (Attached R.A.M.C. man)

Vol 23

ORIGINAL

W A R D I A R Y

- of -

110 th MACHINE GUN COMPANY

- for -

JANUARY 1918

Vol. 24

Army Form C. 2118.

WAR DIARY
or
INTELLIGENCE SUMMARY.
(Erase heading not required.)

Instructions regarding War Diaries and Intelligence Summaries are contained in F. S. Regs., Part II. and the Staff Manual respectively. Title pages will be prepared in manuscript.

Place	Date	Hour	Summary of Events and Information	Remarks and references to Appendices
	1918 Jan.			
LONGAVESNES	1st		Company in Reserve at LONGAVESNES. Time devoted to Training, Cleaning up etc.	
"	2nd		"	
"	3rd		" Operation Orders received to relieve 237th Machine Gun Company in the Right Sector tomorrow.	
"	4th		Relieved 237th M.G.Company in the Right Sector.	
EPEHY	5th		Company in the line. Situation quiet.	
"	6th		Situation quiet except for hostile shelling of the Railway Embankment. Situation quiet except that Railway Embankment was intermittently shelled. Several hostile aeroplanes flew over going in a westerly direction between 4 a.m. and 5 a.m. and 6 a.m. and 7 a.m. The first flight returned about 6 a.m. having apparently dropped bombs on villages in the back areas.	
"	7th		Company in the Right Sector. Situation quiet.	
"	8th		"	
"	9th		" Heavy shelling between 4 p.m. and 6 p.m. Gas shells were sent into EPEHY about 8 p.m.	
"	10th		Company in the Right Sector. Situation normal	
"	11th		" Hostile artillery very active during the past 24 hours. Heavy bombardment on left from 8.30 p.m. to 9.15 p.m. Red and white lights sent up by enemy.	
"	12th		Company in the Right Sector. Very heavy shelling of EPEHY, becoming continuous at 8 p.m. 11th instant and lasting until 3 a.m. to-day. Orders received for tomorrow's relief by 237 M.G.Company.	
"	13th		Company relieved by 237 M.G.Company, Sections on being relieved marching to Company Headquarters at LONGAVESNES.	
LONGAVESNES	14th		Company moved from LONGAVESNES to SAULCOURT WOOD.	
SAULCOURT WOOD	15th 18th		Company in Reserve in Camp at SAULCOURT WOOD. Time devoted to Cleaning up, Kit and spare parts checking, Training and Practice of Corps Defence Scheme.	
"	19th		Company in Training. Two gun teams of Company took over positions from 64th Machine Gun Company at R.19 and R.20.	
"	20th		Orders received to relieve 237 M.G.Company in the Right Sector. Day devoted to packing limbers and cleaning guns and equipment etc ready for the line. "B" Echelon established at SAULCOURT WOOD and Transport Lines at LONGAVESNES.	
"	21st		Relieved 237th Machine Gun Company in the Right Sector.	

Army Form C. 2118.

WAR DIARY
or
INTELLIGENCE SUMMARY.

(Erase heading not required.)

Instructions regarding War Diaries and Intelligence Summaries are contained in F. S. Regs., Part II. and the Staff Manual respectively. Title pages will be prepared in manuscript.

Place	Date	Hour	Summary of Events and Information	Remarks and references to Appendices
EPEHY	1918 Jan. 22nd to 28th		Company in the Line in Right Sector. Situation Quiet. One casualty sustained during this period, No. 107768 Pte MELLARS W. being killed on the 23rd instant.	
"	29th		Relieved by 237th Machine Gun Company, Sections on being relieved marching to Company Headquarters at SAULCOURT WOOD. Two guns remained in the Line at R.19 and R.20 gun positions.	
SAULCOURT WOOD	30th		Company in Reserve at Saulcourt Wood. Day devoted to Cleaning of guns and equipment, checking of kit and gun equipment etc.	
"	31st		Company in Training. The two guns at R.19 and R.20 being relieved to-day by two guns of the 1st M.M.G.Battery	

Vol 24

ORIGINAL

WAR DIARY

- of -

110th MACHINE GUN COMPANY

- for -

FEBRUARY 1918

Vol. 25

Army Form C. 2118.

WAR DIARY
or
INTELLIGENCE SUMMARY.
(Erase heading not required.)

Instructions regarding War Diaries and Intelligence Summaries are contained in F.S. Regs., Part II. and the Staff Manual respectively. Title pages will be prepared in manuscript.

Place	Date	Hour	Summary of Events and Information	Remarks and references to Appendices
SAULCOURT WOOD	1918 Feb. 1st to 6th		Company at Camp at SAULCOURT WOOD. Transport at LONGAVESNES. Time devoted to Training, cleaning and checking of gun equipment, kit inspections, C.O's inspection etc.	
"	7th		Operation Orders issued for the relief of 237th Machine gun Company tomorrow. Company relieved 237 Company in the Right Sector. Company H.Q. at EPEHY, "B" Echelon at SAULCOURT WOOD and Transport at LONGAVESNES.	
EPEHY Right Sector	8th to 14th		Company in the Right Sector during this period. Situation - quiet. Nothing unusual to report.	
"	15th		Relieved by 48th Machine Gun Company. Sections on being relieved proceeding by train to Billets at HAMEL. Relief completed by 9 p.m.	
HAMEL	16th to 21st		Company in Training. First day devoted to Baths, cleaning up etc. Succeeding days - kit inspection, checking of gun equipment and general training. Transport Lines moved from LONGAVESNES to SAULCOURT.	
HAMEL	22nd to 27th		Company in training at HAMEL	
HAMEL	28th	1 p.m.	Orders received br Company to be prepared to move at a moments notice.	
"	"	"	Marched to LONGAVESNES.	

mo 95/2/65/5

110th Brigade.

21st Sivision.

110th TRENCH MORTAR BATTERY

AUGUST 1916.

Army Form C. 2118

Vol 1

WAR DIARY
or
INTELLIGENCE SUMMARY
(Erase heading not required.)

110 TRENCH MORTAR BATTERY

AUGUST 1916

Place	Date	Hour	Summary of Events and Information	Remarks and references to Appendices
	31.7.16	night	Joined Brigade from 3rd Army School of Mortars, having finished refresher course	
	2.8.16		Took over emplacements in J2 Sector. Putting in 3 mortars into defensive positions. Two situated behind CLAUD & CLARENCE CRATERS and one in Nov. Av. to enfilade these crater and No MAN'S LAND	
	3.8.16		Put in a fourth mortar in emplacement close to November Avenue for use retaliatory work.	
	4.8.16			
	5.8.16 to 18.8.16		Repairing and improving of emplacements, cleaning and arranging of ammunition, checking working bearings etc.	
	18.8.16	evening	Took over from 62nd T.M.B emplacements in J1 Sector consisting of two emplacements behind trenches 92, 93 respectively, one for defence and one for retaliation, one in firing line Trench 91. One behind Trench 83 and a hardly finished one adjoining.	
			Disposition of guns altered and are situated as follows :-	
			Position 83 Two mortars for retaliation, and also for defence of trenches 81 – 84	
			" 93 One mortar principally for defence of crater CUTHBERT, available also for retaliation purposes in immediate neighbourhood.	
			" 94 One mortar for defence of CUTHBERT and CLARENCE crater	
			" 95 One mortar for defence of CLAUD crater.	
			" 99 Nov Avenue :- One mortar principally for defence of craters, available also for retaliation purposes in immediate neighbourhood during the day.	

Army Form C. 2118

SHEET 2

WAR DIARY
or
INTELLIGENCE SUMMARY

110 TRENCH MORTAR BATTERY

AUGUST 1916

(Erase heading not required.)

Instructions regarding War Diaries and Intelligence Summaries are contained in F.S. Regs., Part II. and the Staff Manual respectively. Title Pages will be prepared in manuscript.

Place	Date	Hour	Summary of Events and Information	Remarks and references to Appendices
Night	14/5	9.30 PM	In co-operation with Lewis Guns, we fired on a working party in small enemy centres.	London ARRAS 1/10,000 G 6 c 55 . 30
	18-23		A good deal of firing was done in retaliation for rifle grenades. Defensive points commanding enemy saps are now set. Have also received attention.	
	24	9.30 PM	Opened slow fire on crater. This was under our own gun's enfilade fire, the bursting of our fire being to prevent possible occupation of crater, from which enfilade fire could have been brought to bear on raiding party.	
	27	Evening	Special attention was given by one gun to ranging on a rifle grenade post.	
	28	6.30	Site for new emplacement selected and ranged from, also a retaliatory position found and marked. Ranging with long range cartridge is being done from all available emplacements.	
	31		Firing in retaliation to rifle grenade engaged in. At night an enemy sap was fired upon also a new O.P. which is in course of erection. The latter was materially damaged. At midnight slow fire was opened on front line from G 12 a 57.90 to G 6 c 55.10 with the purpose of worrying working parties reported to be out.	

7/9/16

C. F. Lawson Capt
O.C. 110 T M Battery

www.ingramcontent.com/pod-product-compliance
Lightning Source LLC
Chambersburg PA
CBHW081536160426
43191CB00011B/1773